Gettir
Without A Hitch

Getting Hitched Without A Hitch

How to Plan Your Dream Wedding in the Real World

Dona Chernoff Eichner

Andrews McMeel
Publishing

Kansas City

www.andrewsmcmeel.com

00 01 02 03 RDH 10 9 8 7 6 5 4 3 2

Library of Congress Cataloging-in-Publication Data
Eichner, Dona Chernoff.
    Getting hitched without a hitch : how to plan your dream wedding in the real world / Dona Chernoff Eichner.
      p. cm.
    ISBN: 0-8362-6757-5 (pbk)
    1. Weddings—United States—Planning.   2. Wedding etiquette—United States.   I. Title.
    HQ745.E34   1999
    395.2'2—dc21   98-49165
                                              CIP

Design by Holly Camerlinck
Typeset by Top Dog Design

To my future brides: Lucy and Josie

Contents

Acknowledgments

I would like to thank Rick Kot, Betsy Lerner, and Becky Saletan for their early reads, responses, and encouragement.

To my maid of honor, Fern Schapiro, for coming through for me again with a great title.

To Kim Witherspoon and Maria Massie, who were considerate enough to get married while I was working on the book.

To Chris Schillig, years ago a great colleague, and today a great publisher.

To Gideon Weil for his efforts.

To my mother for everything.

Last but not least, to Max, for putting up with me and for his encouragement and support.

Foreword: The Rules

The most important rule is that there *are* no rules; almost everything is flexible and everything is up to you and your fiancé. However, having said that, there are exceptions to every rule.

Etiquette still has a place in this world, but don't get carried away by conventional wisdom. Whatever you think is the right way usually is, just bear in mind that there are a number of prickly areas. There are also many gray areas that aren't just about manners; they have to do with common sense and the desire to maintain a cordial relationship with your family and his.

Traditional weddings haven't changed that much since Emily Post and Amy Vanderbilt wrote their edicts. If you want to know every traditional and often antiquated do and don't, check them out. But if you're like most of us, you've learned to go with the flow. You just need to know which aspects are carved in stone and some guidance in making sensible choices about the rest. In fact, you don't even have to wear white anymore, when odds are you won't even be a virgin!

Here is the top ten list of important rules to help you plan your wedding:

 It's better to laugh than to cry.
Keep your sense of humor, or rent one for the duration. Don't get too stressed out; you won't accomplish anything. In that respect it's just like real life.

2

Get organized.
Make a list of all the things you need to do immediately and get them accomplished early on. You will feel a real sense of accomplishment every time you cross something off your list.

Establish a budget.
Until you know what you can afford to spend on the entire affair, you can't allocate your money properly; and you don't want to blow it all on one piece of the pie.

Don't assume anything.
Get second, third, and fourth opinions from the "experts." Think how long you would shop around for a great pair of shoes. Shouldn't you pay at least that much attention to your wedding?

Talk to him.
Ask your fiancé's opinion for two reasons. One: You don't really want to do anything that he finds absolutely repellent. Two: If something goes wrong, you can blame him later for not talking you out of it.

Don't make new friends.
And don't think you have to invite everyone from your past.

Don't listen to anyone else.
Or more specifically, listen and filter out everything you don't agree with. Don't pay too much attention to other people's advice or you will go crazy!

You get what you pay for.
As much as you want to keep things affordable, don't choose a photographer because he is the cheapest one around. By the same token, don't assume the most expensive one is the best.

Don't rush it.

Don't plan on getting married in four months and expect to have a full-fledged wedding, unless you hire a professional to help you. Hey, Rome wasn't built in a day.

 Stop talking about it.

No one else, including your fiancé, is as fascinated by this as you are. Contrary to popular belief, the world doesn't revolve around your wedding. It should, but it just doesn't. So keep things in perspective.

Congratulations!!! You're engaged. Now for the bad news: You have to plan a wedding. If you don't find this ominous, you're obviously still in the glowing phase of love. But don't worry, that will pass and at some point in this wedding planning process you will consider elopement or calling the whole thing off. It's perfectly natural, everyone does it. I mean everyone *thinks* about it; they don't all actually do it. To be on the safe side, *Getting Hitched* will be here to help you get through it without breaking it off, going broke, or breaking anything.

No matter what your religion, finances, size, or schedule, planning a wedding is overwhelming. And why shouldn't it be? After all, it will probably be (up to this point) the most important day of your life. I'm going on the assumption that this is a first marriage, that you haven't already given birth, and that your sweet sixteen bash can't compare.

All of a sudden you're engaged and by next weekend you have to find a place, unless you want to be engaged for three years. Forget your biological clock ticking, start listening to that nuptial clock. You need help and you hardly know where to turn first. You may pick up one of the popular bridal magazines, thinking that will get you going in the right direction. While there are plenty of great pictures, you can hardly find the articles. You realize that these serve an entirely different purpose; you need something that fills in the details. Maybe not *all* of the details—that would be an encyclopedia—just the important ones. At least by our definition. You've come to the right place.

4 First, some perspective on this wedding business. According to *Bride's* magazine, most engagements last an average of 12.1 months. The median first-time bride is 24.5 years old and her groom is 26.5. According to a recent Census Bureau study, one in every 111 Americans gets married each year. That's close to 2,500,000 weddings a year, from which the wedding industry pulls in approximately $35 billion. With the average wedding costing $17,600, according to *Modern Bride*. In the New York metropolitan area, that figure jumps to $33,600.

Certainly, you're not average, you don't fall into any category, with the possible exception of crazy in love. Which, needless to say, is the most important ingredient of a successful wedding. Though money doesn't hurt either. There are ways to have a fantastic wedding without breaking the bank and that's what we're here for, to guide you through the good times and the bad. The best way to handle this overload is to establish a budget, get organized, and limit your options. Easy for me to say, but not that hard for you to do.

When it comes to weddings, nobody tells you that practice makes perfect, or that each delivery gets easier. With virtually no guidance, but lots of unsolicited advice, you're supposed to get it right the first time. Talk about pressure.

Don't have your parents take out a second mortgage so you can have it all. Guess what? Most of us can't have it all. Some of you will have unlimited funds and if you can't think of anything better to do with your money than blow hundreds of thousands of dollars on a wedding, then all I can say is, am I invited?

I don't want to get mushy or anything, and I'll try not to do it again, but your wedding day is really about love. About the two of you and not about how much it cost. Remember, money can't buy love. At least not the first time around.

Some Ground Rules: I'll assume you are marrying a great guy who is just perfect for you. However, the opposite assumption goes for your families, particularly in the buttinsky mother department. This is not to get down on mothers; I *am* one. However, mothers have a tendency to get a tad excited, especially if you're the only girl or the first to get hitched. After all, they've been thinking about this since the day you were born. Some moms think they are getting married and that they can call all the shots. I'm not good with statistics or graphs, but there is an inverse relationship between the amount of money they are contributing and how often you can tell them to mind their own business. A gentle reminder is certainly in order, about this being *your wedding*. Reminding them who are the stars of this production and who are the supporting players. I'll try to help you navigate this thin gray line between telling them off and not jeopardizing your cash flow.

Keep in mind that this is a very important day for dear old mom and dad. You are their little girl (just a figure of speech). Let them invite their friends; odds are they can afford better gifts than yours anyway. Before you sneer and mumble something about materialism, talk to me *after* the wedding. Believe me, foreplay on your wedding night will consist of opening the envelopes.

A wedding is similar to pregnancy. Approximately nine months of gestation culminates in one of the most amazing days of your life. You're left with a baby to take care of the rest of your life (we're not going to talk about divorce here; pregnancy is bad enough). The major difference is that long before your wedding day, you are pretty much assured of the sex of your baby. You get great presents, a highlight of both occasions. A honeymoon is preferable to a stay in the maternity ward, but in both cases the idea is to stay as long and get as much rest as possible. In both instances, you will have another human being pawing at your body—though your newborn will concentrate mainly on your breasts.

To carry this analogy one step further, I think all women should unite and embrace this philosophy: When you're pregnant, you're allowed to ride a roller coaster of emotions that run the gamut from adorable to psychotic, and everyone just chalks it up to hormones. I would like to make a case for the wedding hormone. If you haven't already noticed, your emotions will be in major flux. One minute you may be daydreaming about the perfect wedding dress and then you're screaming at your fiancé to mind his own business, it's *your wedding!* We all know you will want to kill your intended at some point during

6

this process. Sure it's his wedding, technically. But does he really have the right to invoke his opinions?

This book is for all you gals who have been fantasizing since third grade about a wedding with a dozen bridesmaids wearing dresses in every shade of the rainbow. It's also for you practical women who never thought you would spend that much money on a wedding dress. Until you broke down in tears when you looked in the fitting room mirror (not the same kind of tears as when you try on bathing suits). Because no matter how practical, mature, sensible, or logical you may think you are, odds are you won't maintain your "high standards" when it comes to *your wedding day*. This is an amazing milestone in most of our lives. The truth is we want it to be perfect. This book will help you have the wedding of your dreams. The marriage is up to you.

To quote *The New York Times,* "Weddings have shown themselves to be very resistant to change in a country eagerly promoting gender equality and informality. The ceremony continues to cast the bride in anachronistic, if not demeaning roles: unapproachable princess in a spectacular, impractical gown. Sacrificial virgin in white. Currency handed off from the old patriarchy to a budding one." Okay, so they were wrong about the virgin part, but the rest does resonate. That's why weddings are big business: They are our shot at happily ever after. Can't we actually play make-believe, just this once?

Society perpetuates this fantasy beginning when we are little girls. "Daddy's little princess, what a heartbreaker." Our parents are already marrying us off by the time we're five. My own girls are currently four and six, and have had a few broken engagements. I still have my hopes pinned on one little boy in particular. See what I mean? We joke about it, but isn't there truth in humor? (Not always. Sometimes it's just a cheap ploy for a laugh, but that's another story.)

As much as we believe in equality of the sexes and support women's lib, though we hardly understand what it represents anymore, when it comes to our wedding we want to go the traditional route, at least for part of the ride. What we are not wedded to are all the arcane and archaic etiquette rules. If you listen to the etiquette police, you can lose your mind. The reality is that most of the rules are obsolete, or **7** should be. Within reason, you should do what you want to do. The bride can wear black for all I care, if that's what she wants. Certainly her mom can. If you're old enough and mature enough to get married, you should be sensible enough to know what is important.

During this entire planning process, you will hear many different stories, versions, and suggestions. Listen to them all, filter through them, and pull out the advice that you find relevant. There is a lot of information out there that can actually help make things run more smoothly, efficiently, and economically. So get a notebook, keep a file, and fill it with anything and everything that strikes your fancy. Keep the faith, you will survive. Many brides have walked down that aisle before you and many more will follow. Maintain your perspective and your sense of humor. Believe me, you are going to need it. We're all so happy for you and know you will have the wedding of your dreams.

Drum roll please: *Getting Hitched Without A Hitch.*

1.

A Diamond Is Forever

The diamond engagement ring dates back to fifteenth-century Venice. By the seventeenth century it had become the most popular symbol of betrothal. One of the earliest documented cases was Archduke Maximilian of Austria who popped the question in 1477. But, it's never too early to introduce a little princess to diamonds, as occurred in 1518, when two-year-old Princess Mary, daughter of Henry VIII, was promised to the dauphin of France and got a rock she couldn't play with.

The actual evolution of the engagement ring dates back as early as AD 860, when Pope Nicholas I mandated the ring as a required promise of betrothal. Not just any ring, mind you, but one of precious metal, preferably gold. The premise was that this would show a financial commitment for the groom-to-be. Who says the Catholic church wasn't progressive?

"A diamond is a girl's best friend" and for the amount of money it'll cost, it had better be. This may be your first real introduction to the fact that you are a couple now and the money he is spending is, figuratively (I hope) speaking, yours too! Gone are the days when you didn't think about where the money was coming from. Think about the fact that this is only the first of many large expenses (even if your parents are paying

9

10 for the wedding), from all the extra wedding stuff to a honeymoon to setting up a home together.

I don't want to scare you, I just want to provide the first of many reality checks. We all know you're worth more than "two months' salary," no matter how much he makes. Just keep things in perspective. Set a budget. This is the first of many skills that will come in handy when planning a wedding. This may also be the first of many times that you will blow your budget, but it's a good idea to have a jumping-off point. This is also the first of the LIFE LESSONS you will be introduced to in this book. These lessons will serve you well and be recurring themes in your life.

Back to basics. Deal with a reputable and honest jeweler. Easier said than done? If you do your homework (another LIFE LESSON that will come in handy when planning this wedding), you can avoid the pitfalls. Talk to your friends, your parents, and if there is someone whose ring you admire, them too. You may be surprised to find that your mom's best friend has a cousin in the jewelry business.

At this point, many of you may be thinking, isn't this *his* job? Talk about your major LIFE LESSON. If he intends to surprise you with the ring, at least show him what you like and steer him in the right direction. I personally don't think it's a great idea to purchase something so important and expensive without some discussion between you. Don't assume that he can make this decision solo because he knows your taste. Please, don't assume that he has a clue; he is a man after all (a LIFE LESSON you must have learned by now).

You can always pick out a ring together and he can surprise you with the actual proposal. Wouldn't you prefer that? Instead of being surprised with a ring you don't really like and pretending you do, so you don't hurt his feelings? And by the way, if you can't afford the diamond of your dreams (stop dreaming), there are many alternatives that I'll talk about later.

Shopping for an engagement ring can be an overwhelming experience. To lessen your ignorance and apprehension, there are some basic facts, you should know about *diamond* rings.

THE FIVE C's

Cut, carat, color, clarity, and certification. Six if you count cost. The International Gemological Institute recommends spending two to three months' salary on a ring. And why shouldn't they? It's their business. The average cost of an engagement ring is estimated at just over $2,800 (though I have seen lower estimates). I don't know if that includes tax. Which, by the way, you can avoid if you live in a state without sales tax and you buy the ring in a state that does. They can send you the ring (insured). They won't send you an empty box anymore, because of pesky government regulations.

You can also sometimes avoid tax by paying in cash. Some "experts" say that jewelers want cash because by doing so you relinquish your rights. I don't understand this, since you're not about to pay without some kind of receipt and certification (more about this later).

Cut

This refers to the diamond's shape and its facets. While we only really care about the shape, any good jeweler knows the importance of a proper cut. A good cut is responsible for the sparkle and shine of the stone. This is the most critical aspect in your choice of a stone, since a smaller, brilliant stone is superior to a larger, dull stone. (LIFE LESSON: Quality, not quantity.)

While we understand this, we still only really care about the actual shape. There are seven major choices. The round cut is the most popular, comprising almost 70 percent of all sales, followed by the marquis at 20 percent, and the rest in the order listed.

ROUND or brilliant cut: This is the most brilliant, as it best reflects the light.

MARQUIS: Looks like an oval with points; think a football, slightly deflated.

OVAL: Do you really need me to describe it?

EMERALD: A rectangular shape with slightly rounded corners.

PEAR: Looks like a teardrop; I guess a pear sounds better.

TRILLION: Three-sided cut, variations on triangles.

SQUARE: Princess is a square with sharp, pointed corners. Radiant is also square, with rounded corners.

Once you've chosen the shape (mine is a pear, since you asked), you will learn that most men are concerned with buying the largest diamond they can afford. And are not all that concerned with the other equally important aspects. Isn't it shocking that most men consider size the most important thing? Gee, where have I heard that before?

Not to say that in some regards, we don't think bigger is better. But unlike men, we tend to appraise the overall package, if you know what I mean.

Carat

Back to diamonds. . . . The size of a diamond is measured by carats. One carat equals 200 milligrams and is measured by points. One carat is equal to 100 points, so a diamond that is 1 and ¼ is considered 1.25 carats. Who said women aren't good at math? Just give us something pertinent.

Obviously size increases price, but don't sacrifice cut, color, and clarity for carats. If you can't afford a diamond solitaire, consider a smaller one with baguettes on the side, and those don't necessarily have to be diamonds.

Color

In this case, colorless is king and it scales down to near colorless; faint yellow; very light yellow; and light yellow. This sliding scale is rated from D to Z. I guess they started with D in honor of diamond. Most affordable diamonds show traces of color. In fact, D to G are undetectable to the naked eye, so most diamonds you should consider are in the G to M range. The near colorless goes from G to J, making this group the biggest seller in the marketplace.

Clarity

This grading system refers to the inclusions (imperfections or blemishes) in the stone. Their size and type determine the diamond's value.

The ratings range from:

- Fl: Flawless.
- IF: Internally flawless, minor surface blemishes, not visible to the naked eye.
- VVSI/VVS2: Very, very slight inclusions.
- VSI/VS2: Very slight inclusions.
- SII/SI2: Slight inclusions, may become visible to the naked eye.
- II: Imperfect, visible to the naked eye, but may not affect its brilliance.
- I2/I3: Imperfect and visible to the naked eye.

Not surprisingly, most diamonds sold fall into the SI grades.

Certification

This is the proof of a diamond's identity and grade. Every jeweler should supply this information, from a graduate gemologist. The customer has the option of requesting—and paying for—a grading and certificate from a recognized gemological institute. If the store won't supply a written appraisal, do not purchase your ring there. Ever wonder why it's such a good deal?

You should always get an independent appraisal to authenticate the stone's value, which you will also need for insurance purposes. Most diamond rings are included in a rider on your home or apartment insurance.

A list of reputable appraisers is available from the American Gem Society. If you determine that your jeweler misrepresented the quality of your diamond, contact The Jewelers Vigilance Committee at 1-800-JOINJVC.

Never buy diamonds in a setting, always view them loose. A mounting can camouflage imperfections. Obviously, antique rings are

14   an exception. If you are not sure about something, ask! Ask a million questions and if the jeweler is not helpful, go somewhere else. There are plenty of fish in this sea.

Once you find something you like, don't obsess about all of these factors. If you wanted a stone in the G to J range and this one is an L, if it looks good to you, that's what's important. These are just guidelines, so you are prepared and it doesn't all sound like gibberish to you. It's vital to make an educated choice, but don't be dictated to by a formula.

A STONE OF A DIFFERENT COLOR WILL SHINE JUST AS SWEETLY

Diamonds may be a girl's best friend, but you can never have enough friends. If colored gemstones are good enough for European royalty, they are good enough for us. However, there are certain considerations, if you follow this path.

The major difference between diamonds and other gemstones is that the color is the most important factor. The most popular gems for engagement rings are sapphire, ruby, and emerald, in that order.

> **SAPPHIRE** represents sincerity, truth, and faithfulness. Not bad qualities in a marriage. It is second to the diamond in its hardness and durability.

> **RUBY** indicates passion, with its fiery red color. It is equal to sapphire in hardness.

> **EMERALD** promises fertility and love. It is much softer than sapphire and ruby, and therefore less appropriate for daily wear.

While diamonds are a controlled market, the price variations in colored stones can vary greatly, so it's very important to shop around. If you can't afford one of the more popular stones, consider a more unusual variety. It's all about supply and demand. Find a jeweler who's knowledgeable and has a substantial selection, with a varied range of loose stones. Contrast and compare them, never buy without seeing it for yourself.

Buying an engagement ring is indeed an overwhelming proposition, as is getting engaged, for that matter. But you can overcome your trepidation with some facts and time. Which is more than I can say for the actual wedding. (Just kidding!)

Not to beat a dead horse, but . . . If your boyfriend wants to surprise you and you implicitly trust him, then you are either a) very young, b) hopelessly in love, or c) extremely lucky. For the rest of us, it would be a good idea to show him what you like. Go into jewelry stores together, cut out pictures from magazines, stop a woman on the street (depending on where you live) and point her ring out to him. Make sure he gets it, before you get stuck with something you are not happy with.

Some women don't want an engagement ring. I didn't, but my husband had to go the traditional route and I must admit I was happy to have it. Though truth be told, I never liked the setting; it was too high. So I didn't wear it for over ten years and finally had it reset. Your tastes change considerably, so why can't your setting?

Others can't afford it or think their money may be better spent elsewhere. There are alternatives. See if your grandmother's ring is collecting dust in some safe deposit box. You may love it as is or want to reset the stone. Even before you shop around, ask your mom/his mom if there is a shot at a family heirloom. There are plenty of simple rings, without stones. And, of course, there are beautiful antique rings. The only consideration here is that if you plan on wearing them with a wedding band, make sure they will go together. And, if you don't want a ring, that's perfectly fine. Just be prepared for everyone's eyes to dart to your left hand when you announce your engagement, expecting to see the ring.

If you're like the majority of women, you will want an engagement ring. Look at it as an investment. Diamond prices have consistently increased, approximately 7 percent per year.

Oh, one more piece of advice. Try not to stare at your ring while you are driving or doing something that requires your attention and full concentration, like operating heavy machinery. You'll be surprised at how much time you can waste, admiring the beauty of your ring. Happy daydreams!

Why Does Everyone Make Fun of Martha Stewart?

Do you remember when you were a little girl, fantasizing with your friends about your wedding? Luckily for us, grown-up gals can continue to fantasize and daydream, courtesy of all the bridal magazines out there, and the queen of fantasy: Martha Stewart. Don't get me wrong, these magazines contain a lot of useful information hidden among the gorgeous pictures of stunning, skinny women modeling bridal gowns that cost as much as a car. Pictures of sunsets on honeymoon cruises around the world. China patterns for twelve that cost as much as the down payment on your new apartment.

While there are no statistics on the subject, every bride-to-be that I have ever come across has bought at least one of these magazines. What better way is there to absorb everything? This is the ultimate in Cliff Notes. You are a dry sponge (figuratively speaking) and trying to soak up as much as possible. And there's plenty to choose from. Check out your local newsstand and you can be an elegant bride, a modern bride, an Alaskan bride, not to mention a blushing bride. I hold Martha up as the Queen Bee of wedding hoopla, but there are many others buzzing

18 around. The list of national bridal magazines is staggering, plus there's one for every state.

Then there are the bridal faires. Yes there is an "e"; I guess they don't want to be confused with a carnival. Though the atmosphere is not dissimilar. Imagine that one of the magazines has come to life. Everywhere you turn, someone is hawking something. You can plan your entire wedding on the spot and you will certainly feel the pressure to do so. Just don't act on this impulse. Bring a pad and pencil and take notes. Take pamphlets, take handouts, take anything that's free. There is no soft selling going on, and why should there be? They are playing to a captive audience. It's a kind of one-stop shopping. Everything from bands and DJs to florists and photographers are on site. While I don't recommend going there cold and making decisions on the spot, it is a great place to go window-shopping. The added bonus is that you can win door prizes and assorted contests, so you can get something to cover that entrance fee. Which can often be avoided, if you preregister.

Collect all the literature, rip pages out of the magazines. If you see a fabulous hairdo in the pages of a regular magazine, throw that in your folder too. Many florists suggest doing the same with flowers, center-pieces, and arrangements you admire. Remember, a picture is worth a thousand words. As far as the bridal magazines go, don't worry about ripping out a page with useful information on the back; odds are it's another advertisement. And that, my friend, is the true mixed blessing of all these magazines: great visualization, but little information. For the cost of two magazines, you could pick up a useful book to guide you. Oh, I see you already have. We don't have all the fancy pictures, just the facts.

Another important service that these magazines provide is that they give you a mini stress test. Let me explain. In virtually every magazine (and the bulk of the books in this section) are planners. Their purpose is to make you feel as if you are way behind. Regardless of when you started. These time frames do serve a purpose, by showing you a schedule fit for an aspiring Stepford wife. The reality is that everyone is in a different situation, with different priorities, finances, and abilities. So don't let these time lines drive you crazy; they are not carved in stone.

Another important thing to remember is that it's *your* wedding, it's individual, and you don't have to make anyone happy besides you and your fiancé (at times he's questionable). **19**

There was a great line on the television show, *Everybody Loves Raymond*. They did a flashback episode, when Ray and Debra first became engaged. She immediately moves into high planning gear and pulls out her stack of information and when he questions her, she replies that she has been planning this wedding since she was twelve. Ray was just the last piece of the puzzle. Ain't it the truth. No matter how independent, career minded, or individualistic we may think we are, the truth is that every little girl has dreamed about her wedding. My daughters are four and six, and they even talk about who they are going to marry. For better or worse, that's how our society works, so we may as well cave in to all this pressure.

Now do you understand the evolution of Martha? She is performing a public service and filling a vast void in our lives. Actually, she is appealing to the very small percentage that can actually carry off the advice she offers. Why would we want to learn how to remove a ketchup stain from our fine linen and then reuse the ketchup? We are not deluded enough to actually think we can participate, but it's fun to watch. We don't aspire to be Miss America, but would we consider missing the show?

3.

All in the Family

It's weird enough being a member of your own dysfunctional family, let alone becoming part of another. Not to sound like a Pollyanna, but, you may as well approach your new family with enthusiasm. Potentially more than your fiancé does. I mean, toward his own family. What's the alternative? There are plenty of reasons not to get along, down the road. It's much easier to maintain a cordial relationship with them when you keep it superficial. In some ways, you are in your "honeymoon" period. It's only going to get more difficult after the marriage, when the gloves come off, or at least until you redeem yourself by producing an heir.

Many women feel that that is the actual point when they are truly accepted into his family. Now that the "ties that bind" are irrevocable, they realize that they have no choice. But I'm jumping ahead, hopefully more than nine months ahead.

You're plenty stressed out trying to plan this wedding (like I need to remind you), and if you're not, you will be. So my advice is to go against conventional wisdom. Do not truly treat them like family until after the wedding. Think about how you treat your own family. How

22 you speak to them. How you tell them to mind their own business. How you tell them to @##$@^$ and other unprintable things. Can't that wait? I don't mean to imply for a second that you don't love your immediate family. Obviously you do, that's how you get away with treating each other like this. No one else would ever stand for it.

You know how you are always kinder to your friends' parents. How their father's jokes are never as painful or as embarrassing as dear old dad's. How it's not as mortifying when their mother wears peds with open-toed sandals. I think you know what I mean.

Most experts I've come across say you should adopt his family as if it were your own. As if. Offer them your unconditional love. I'm no expert, but I think that's crazy. How are we expected to feel this way about virtual strangers? Excuse me, but we've spent our whole lives with our own families. Can't we gently test the waters with his?

As far as the wedding planning goes, include them if they so desire. But, don't let them feel comfortable enough that they think they can get really involved. It's one thing to ask them what shade of mauve they like, but it's entirely another matter for them to speak when they are not spoken to. If you are brave enough to ask a question, you have to listen to the answer, so think before you speak. Seriously, take things slow. It's a bumpy enough ride planning a wedding. There's plenty of time to bond after the honeymoon.

Try to get to know them, outside of all the wedding hoopla. Some of you lucky gals have already bonded with his family, before the wedding. That's great. But if you aren't one of these dozen, don't sweat it. If you have already connected to his family and they make you miserable, just take a deep breath, put down that drink, and keep reading.

Now is a perfect time to get your fiancé involved. If he truly loves you (I'm not touching that line), he may not automatically take your side, but he can act as a buffer between you and his _____ (fill in the blank). I'll address specific mother-in-law (not to mention mother) issues, in the next chapter.

You'll hear and read a lot of mumbo jumbo about your relationship with your in-laws and in-siblings. (I don't think that's a word, but it should be.) Like most things in life that all these self-help, relationship experts fail to mention, the logical solution is usually common sense and courtesy. You know, do unto others. . . . Or keep biting your tongue.

Don't think you have to love everyone in his family, or vice versa. Truth be told, most people wouldn't be so crazy about their own, if they weren't related. But whatever you do, don't let your feelings destroy or poison his relationship with his family.

Other scenarios may present themselves. You may be the daughter they never had. The sister she always wanted. They may want to smother you with love and affection. Go shopping to make up for twenty-five years of not being able to buy those adorable girl outfits. Phone calls, lunches . . . I think you get the idea.

The easiest way (easy for me to say) is to try and set parameters. Include your new extended family when you can, and hopefully they will appreciate it. If you think it would make her feel like she died and went to heaven, then bring his mom along on one of your wedding gown trips. Believe me, the experience is strange and overwhelming, with or without her. Just don't let them control your life.

By the same token, don't expect them to want to share every moment with you. Or hear about every detail of the wedding planning. Face it, your fiancé doesn't even want to hear it.

HELLO MUDDA, HELLO FADDA

One of the trickiest, unresolved areas is what to call your future in-laws (to their face, I mean). I know many people who, after ten years plus of marriage, still haven't addressed their in-laws by any name. If you can hold out until you have kids, you can always resort to Grandma and Grandpa, or any variation thereof.

I read an article in a bridal magazine that presented a woman whose compromise was to call her father-in-law "Big Daddy." A name that is really low down on my list of possibilities. May I take the liberty of suggesting it be just as far down on yours?

If you're uncomfortable with Mom and Dad, don't use them. You

24   may grow into it or you may not. Don't sweat it. In the meantime, it's perfectly acceptable to call them by their first name or whatever nickname they choose.

If you're not sure and are uncomfortable, discuss this issue with them. Better yet, have your fiancé ask them what they are comfortable with. Of course, if their response is Mom and Dad, feel free to ignore them. If it ever comes up, tell them that their son never mentioned it to you. Seriously, just let them know *gently,* that you are not really comfortable calling them Mom or Dad just yet. Tell them you need some time to adjust.

Try to find something positive about his family. Look again. For 99 percent of you, there is something worthwhile. If all else fails, think about how much they love your intended. They do, don't they? When you've reached the end of your rope, imagine yourself in their shoes. It's not easy giving up their little boy. A daughter is a daughter for the rest of your life but a son is only a son until he takes a wife. When boys fly the coop, they are, usually, out of there. Let her know she's not losing a son, she's gaining a daughter. This may be the best piece of news she has ever received. If it's the worst, check out the next chapter.

4.

Mommy Dearest

Many of you have a wonderful relationship with your mother, and assume you will have an equally cordial one with your future mother-in-law (MIL). I hope that's true, but for others this is a pipe dream. Even if you get along with both ladies most of the time, during the stress of the wedding planning, relationships can get a bit strained.

With the exception of your fiancé, your mother and/or his mother will become your primary candidates for most annoying human being on the planet, if they're not already. You will soon learn one of the basic tenets of any wedding: Just as you don't think the wedding is really for your fiancé, your mom doesn't really think it's for you. Especially if your parents are paying for it, and it's even more offensive when they're not but still want to invite everyone they know. Not everyone—just the neighbors, the office, relatives you thought were dead (and others you wish were), and anyone who ever invited them to any occasion. In almost every wedding, the "grown-ups" outnumber the kids. You're one of the kids, by the way.

The guest list falls under the adage, "You can't fight city hall." It's one of the true tests of diplomacy and compromise. Henry Kissinger never had to deal with this kind of aggravation. *Don't stress out.* If you could be objective for just a moment, you would honestly understand much of your mom's list. The ones you are openly hostile to, except most relatives, you can delete. Besides, it's almost traditional for parents to monopolize the party. Look at the bright side: You'll do it to your kids some day. Odds are that your parents' friends will have more money to spend on your wedding gifts than your friends. Is that materialistic? Mea culpa! But don't think you won't be opening those envelopes with relish.

Try to respect their opinions. For some reason, our mothers and our mothers-in-law can push all our buttons. While we may love them more than anyone in the world, they can also drive us crazier than anyone in the world. As for your future mother-in law, attempt to get to know her and find out what her pet peeves are. There are numerous stories about horrible mothers-in-law, but there are good ones too. I don't know why you don't hear about those.

One of my friends doesn't have a great relationship with her husband's mom, and it started with the wedding planning. Apparently, they had a big fight over what the MIL was wearing to the wedding. Diane wanted her to wear a certain color. Her MIL said she found the perfect dress, but not in that color, and insisted on wearing it. Well, Diane found out that she had the dress custom made and obviously could have used the color Diane wanted. On the wedding day, the wedding consultant went over to the MIL to say how lucky she was and what a lovely daughter-in-law she was getting. The MIL from hell muttered something about her not being good enough for her son. Well, Diane heard this and had a cow. She was so upset she almost didn't go through with the wedding. Then she had an epiphany—one all you women with a similar problem should bear in mind. The best revenge, and the one thing she could do to piss off his mom, was to marry the crown prince. That cheered her up and she marched happily down the aisle.

The truth is that the moms can wear any color they want, though they should take into consideration the wedding party colors. They should also respect the formality of the bridal party. If the girls are wearing evening gowns, they too should wear floor-length. Black is a hot color for wedding parties, but many mothers are uncomfortable wearing **27** black at their children's wedding. Unless, of course, it's the mother-in-law from hell who looks at this as a somber occasion. Etiquette experts concur and say black doesn't belong. I disagree. Today black goes every-where and anywhere, from kids to mothers of the bride. Another tech-nicality is that both mothers shouldn't wear the same color, and tradi-tionally the mother of the bride gets first dibs. Please, is this what we should be worrying about? Who cares if they wear the same color? The same dress, on the other hand, is an entirely different matter. So the bride's mother is supposed to let the groom's mom know what she has chosen. I don't know the rules, but if she waits until the last minute then I guess anything goes.

You can dress her up, but you can't take her out. What they wear is only one problem area. Let's discuss your own mom first. As usual, there are extreme situations. You call her with the big news and even though you woke her from a sound sleep she begins a recitation of what she has to do and when you can help her. By the next day, she has set up appoint-ments with five different caterers. You can either a) get caught up in her fervor, b) tell her to slow down, she's giving you a headache, or c) resent her involvement. Unless you truly don't want her participation, consider the first two choices. At the other end of the spectrum is the mom who puts you on hold during your big announcement since she's been waiting to get through to PSE&G on the other line. Given the choices, wouldn't you rather have an active, enthusiastic mom? I realize there's a happy medium, but you may not have that option.

You may have been fantasizing about your wedding since you were a little girl, but here's a news flash! Your mom beat you to it. Mom's a few years up on you in this fantasy. I know it's ridiculous, but as I worked on this book, I couldn't help but imagine my daughters going through it. I realize they have to get through kindergarten first, but this is much more entertaining.

Besides, the inalienable right to butt in comes with being your mom! Doesn't her (their) money buy anything else? When else would you hand over thousands and thousands of dollars, and not have a say

28   in how it's spent? Besides college. Just remind your mom that this is not a complete dictatorship, and you'd like to cast the deciding vote.

Having grown up with this woman (I assume), you should have a pretty fair idea of how she will react. Don't expect them to change, not even on your wedding day. If they are manipulative control freaks, why should *your* wedding day change anything? Almost all the brides I spoke with expected their moms to rise to the occasion, to put their feelings aside and fully support their daughter. Virtually all of them were disappointed. Don't have unrealistic expectations (another LIFE LESSON.)

Unfortunately, there is little correlation between her involvement in the wedding and her feelings about the groom-to-be. One might think that the only good part of her not liking him is that she'd wash her hands of the entire matter. Guess again.

My friend Fran has a mother from hell. She sticks her nose into everything and drives everybody crazy. She always has and she always will. While she was no big fan of her daughter's intended, the odds were overwhelming that nobody would be good enough. On the flip side, Fran's mother-in-law was apathetic. She couldn't have cared less. Just send her an invitation and she'd show up.

It's funny, but in some ways this was even more annoying. Didn't she care? Wasn't any of this important enough to have an opinion about? Wasn't Fran the daughter she never had? If you merged these two, you'd have the perfect mom, but this isn't a fairy tale. Nothing and no one is perfect and you'll be in for quite a fall if you have preconceived notions of anyone's behavior. By the way, Fran has been married for two years and I called to ask for some stories about her mother's frantic behavior during her wedding planning. Surprisingly, she couldn't remember a thing. All the times her mom drove her insane, all the screaming matches and threats never to speak to the other were forgotten. The lesson here is that you remember the good parts, so focus on that when the going gets rough. It's easy for me to say, since you're the one going through it. It's what our mothers have been telling us for years, "Take our advice, we've lived through it." Roll with the punches and call your shots. Don't make mountains out of molehills. If you only

fight when it's worth fighting for, you'll win a lot more battles. (I don't **29**
know if you're counting, but that's five clichés in a row.)

Planning a wedding is not a justifiable defense for matricide (yet).
Given our current legal system, I wouldn't be surprised if a test case
comes up soon. My personal favorite is when I called my mother to tell
her I found a wedding dress. Her response was "Can you wear it again?"
I think I shrieked something like "If I got married again!" But it's all a
bit blurry. Does it go without saying that she didn't accompany me on
any of the dress excursions? Did I mention that I'm her only daughter?
As a mother, I can't imagine missing that opportunity, but that's just not
my mother's bag. On the plus side, she hardly butted in on any of the
wedding planning. I tell you this story not just because it's comical or to
humiliate my mom, but rather to illustrate a point. Everyone marches to
the beat of a different drummer. It doesn't mean they love you any less.

Charlotte's mother was always a piece of work, and her wedding
was no exception. There were skirmishes throughout, but the best one
came on the actual wedding day. That morning Charlotte had arranged
for a hair and makeup guy to prepare the wedding party and her mom,
as well as herself. Time was getting tight and since Charlotte's hairstyle
was much more time-consuming, the stylist had the nerve to focus his
attention on the bride before moving on to her mom. Who, incidentally,
needed about ten minutes of blow-drying. Her mom whispered (at the
top of her lungs) to the maid of honor that she wasn't going to the wedding. After a screaming match about that, the stylist got to her mom
with time to spare. Needless to say, her mother has complained ever
since about how she looks in the pictures. Charlotte mistakenly thought
her mother would miraculously transform her personality for the wedding day. If she had been thinking straight, she never would have invited
her mom to take part in the beauty session. She should have arranged to
meet her at the church, knowing full well that the less time they spent
together beforehand, the better.

At least you can tell your mother how you feel. You're still supposed to be polite to his. The best you can do is vent your frustrations at
your guy and possibly suggest that he reason with his dear old mom. If

30 you have a good relationship with his dad, and his dad has a good relationship with his wife, then maybe he can do the dirty work for you. Better yet, if you have a future sister-in-law who speaks the same language, she can deal with her mom—she has much more experience. I think the last alternative is for you to confront her yourself. If she's that out of control, it's probably going to make matters worse and possibly create even more friction.

The underlying theme here is that your mom loves you and his mom loves him, though she may not love her child's intended, yet. No matter what, the overwhelming majority want what's best for their kids. They don't want to be shut out of the most important day of their lives. Can you blame them? Talk to them, let them be involved. They may even have a good suggestion or a creative idea. Either mom may be happy making calls, checking prices. This will make your life easier and hers happier.

Pick your fights, don't obsess over everything. Try to go with the flow. It's one less headache for you and ultimately a lot less stressful. Treat your mother as you would like to be treated. Put yourself in her shoes for just a minute. Then take a deep breath and relax, and it couldn't hurt to bite your tongue every once in a while.

5.

The Wedding Party

With any luck, you have a sister you love and so does he. And all your close friends will be in their ninth month of pregnancy at your wedding. No fights or agonizing decisions here. Yeah, right. For the other 99.999 percent of you, this is one of your earliest and biggest hurdles.

The easiest scenario is to only include siblings and their spouses. Of course, if there are six brothers between you and nary a sister in sight, then you're back to scratch. Not only do you have to choose your girlfriends, you may have to limit his buddies. There is no law that states there has to be an equal amount of ushers and bridesmaids. I'm sorry, I think it looks ridiculous if it's hugely imbalanced. Somehow the wedding photos of two bridesmaids and twelve groomsmen don't look quite right.

Here are a few ground rules:

 You don't need to have an equal number of guys and gals.
(It's not a square dance.)

 You can mix genders.
If your best friend is a guy, he should be in the wedding party. He could certainly be on your side for the pictures,

31

32

but let's call him an usher for argument's sake. I don't know the protocol for inviting him to the shower.

When in doubt, choose family.
You never have to defend a decision if it's a relative. I'm not talking about a third cousin. Even if you aren't all that close to your sister now, you will probably regret it later on if you don't include her.

Choose attendants who are your good friends today.
Just because you were in someone's wedding party five years ago, if you no longer keep in touch you're not obliged to return the favor. Growing up, you may have promised your best friend next door that she would be your maid of honor. Get over it.

Don't pressure anyone into being an attendant.
If someone is not a close friend, don't assume they want this responsibility and expense (read: burden), especially as the maid of honor.

When in doubt, keep it small.
This is a good mantra to repeat throughout your planning. I believe there is a direct proportion between the bride's age and the number of attendants. When we were kids we fantasized about a dozen bridesmaids, but in reality we drop a gal every two years or so. The older we get, the smaller this ensemble becomes.

Choose children wisely and try to limit it to family.
If you are using your friends' children, pick the cutest ones (I'm half-kidding). Definitely pick those who can behave and walk down the aisle without freaking out. No kid is cute enough to pull off a screaming tantrum in the middle of your ceremony.

Don't feel guilty.

Don't feel guilty about your choices, and don't let your friends or family make you feel guilty. (Another LIFE LESSON to remember down the road.) You may bruise a few egos, but if you have your reasons and if they are really your friends, they will understand. I only had a maid of honor and best man, so I had my brothers and some close friends sit at our table during the reception.

 Immediately acknowledge those left out.

You know who I mean. If you were just in a friend's wedding, but have too much family to include her in yours, explain it to her. Don't assume she won't be hurt. This is mostly a girl thing. I've never noticed that guys really care if they are involved or not.

 There are no formal rules.

There are no formal rules (though there should be about the attire), except that you must have two witnesses. You can have two maids of honor; your mother can be your matron of honor. I never thought about it, but although it's not uncommon to see a dad as the best man I've never seen a mom as matron of honor. She's smart enough not to want to be a matron. Hey, if she's your best friend and a willing participant, you go girl.

Before you ask anyone else, talk to your fiancé and decide if you want a large wedding party or a more intimate one. Just remember, if your friends are really your friends, they'll understand. I can't say the same for your relatives.

The simplest option is just having a best man and a maid of honor. As I said, you only need two witnesses and someone to hold your bouquet and the rings. The rest is just window dressing. I'm not sure I would recommend the royal style, where the entire wedding party is

34 comprised of children. Though I wonder, why are they so much better behaved than commoners?

Nowhere in the classified ads, would you stumble upon one like this:

> Bride-to-be seeks woman willing to assist a self-absorbed, crazed person in planning a wedding. Willing to wear horrific yet expensive dress which wouldn't be caught dead in otherwise. Responsibilities include, but are not limited to, buying engagement gift, planning shower and buying gift, buying wedding gift, buying shoes that you won't wear again. Some travel may be required, and must absorb all costs incurred. Be willing to hang out with drunk buddy of the groom and expose yourself to embarrassment of catching the bouquet, and allowing unfamiliar lech to put garter up your thigh. Assist bride before and during the entire process. Must be cheerful, supportive, and enjoy posing for pictures. Compensation involves some form of inexpensive jewelry.

Okay, maybe that's not realistic, nobody would run an ad that long. Seriously, doesn't this ring a bell? As the bride-to-be, consider it your wake-up call. Put yourself in her place—you've probably been there once or twice already or you may be in the future. What goes around, comes around. Talk to the lucky gals who should be flattered and honored to be in your wedding—just don't push it. Take their finances into account, as well as their feelings.

If you think you've seen your share, check this out. Rebecca Whitlinger, a five-time bridesmaid, was tired of spending her money on dresses that were "usually some impossible hue with dyed shoes to match." So she put her $180 dress from a 1988 wedding to good use. She wore it in front of the White House and the Eiffel Tower, for her driver's license photo, not to mention skiing, white-water rafting, volleyball, and voting. Who says you can't get your money's worth out of a "garish, off-the-shoulder gown, with a gold sequined bodice and gold lamé skirt"?

It also got her a spread in *People* and, according to the article, the disdain of the bride in question, not to mention the mother of the bride. Some people just can't take a joke. When Rebecca finally walks down that aisle, let's see if she remembers.

That's one of the weirdest parts of the entire wedding process. You think you won't make the same mistakes or spend a ton of money, but some magical or satanical transformation comes over you when it's your turn.

According to *Bride's,* 22 percent of wedding parties are comprised of four bridesmaids, four ushers, and two children. When you choose whom to honor, bear in mind that besides the financial strain, they also assume additional obligations. While many of them are optional, some are necessary to assure a well-run wedding.

First a little background info. The history of the bridal party extends to the ancient Greeks. Then, most brides were approximately sixteen years old and the bridesmaids were the elder stateswomen (you know, the twenty-five-year-olds) who were sharing their experiences with the young virgins (in the literal and figurative sense). These old goats were also included so their fertility and married bliss would rub off on the bride and keep away evil spirits.

These roles have since evolved:

Maid/matron of honor

The only distinction between the two is that maid refers to a single woman and matron to a married one. As either a sister, relative, or dear friend, this lucky gal is asked to assume many responsibilities. The most important one is being totally supportive of the bride:

- If you don't like the groom, you must pretend you do.
- You must accompany the bride on numerous wedding gown excursions.
- If your protests go unrecognized, you must ultimately pretend to love her gown.
- You must pick a dress that she likes (even though she ignored you), and that you can live with.

36

- You must plan a shower and try to get the other gals in the wedding to help financially and otherwise.
- On the wedding day, you must assist the bride in every way. From last-minute makeup touch-ups to straightening out the veil and train for her walk down the aisle.
- You must keep a checklist with all the pertinent wedding information. It couldn't hurt to keep a cell phone nearby or some change for the phone. (Unless she has a wedding consultant, which is an entirely separate chapter. It may not be a bad shower gift to hire one for the day!)
- Smile inanely for all the photographs.
- Dance with all the groom's loser friends.
- Never complain to the bride.

Now do you understand, why they call it *maid* of honor? Hopefully, you can still have a good time, when you're not too busy helping the bride go to the bathroom in her wedding dress or fending off repeated queries of, "When is it going to be your turn?" After all, you can always retort, "When my boyfriend gets out of jail." That serves the dual purpose of shutting them up and avoiding any possible fix-ups.

Bridesmaids

They have lesser responsibilities. However, they have the awesome job of finding a dress that:

- Looks good on them.
- Looks good (but not as good) on the other bridesmaids.
- The bride likes.
- Doesn't cost an arm and a leg, and, in a perfect world,
- They can actually wear again.

This assumes that the one saving grace of being the maid of honor is that she doesn't have to match the rest of the party. (More about this and other dress details later.)

Of course, these gals do have to be supportive and helpful to the bride, especially on her wedding day. (For that matter, shouldn't everyone?) Help with the shower and think of clever party games. On the big day, if the maid of honor is responsible for being the point person or troubleshooter, they can and should all pitch in to help her. One bridesmaid can be responsible for the flower delivery. A bride I know had someone sign for the boxes, but in the rush of getting ready that morning nobody thought to open them up. When they did get around to it, half the flowers were dead. Not exactly what you want to deal with. If someone had checked while the delivery person was still there, they would have had a real person to deal with rather than arguing over the phone and being put on hold.

Bestman/groomsmen

They have certain duties as well—not that your fiancé will think about this, so it's also your responsibility to prepare the boys.

The best man's history dates back to AD 200 in Northern Europe. In those days, a male companion assisted "the groom" in seizing a young girl who strayed from the safety of her community. Since reprisals from her family often occurred, he hung around, armed, throughout the ceremony. For this task they required the strongest or *best* man for the job. Well, times have changed. His role is much less burdensome than his female counterpart, but basically breaks down as follows:

- In the eyes of the groom, his major responsibility is to plan the bachelor party.
- In the eyes of the bride, his major responsibility is to make sure the groom survives the bachelor party, doesn't become totally inebriated, doesn't drive home, and doesn't have anything to do with the hookers.
- The best man should help with the formalwear arrangements. He usually picks up the groom's tux and returns it, promptly, after the big day.
- Aid and assist the groom. Since they usually have no other responsibility other than showing up on time and well groomed, that basically entails keeping him from getting cold feet.

38

- Drive the groom to the ceremony (odds are he doesn't need to have his car handy). If he is transporting the couple to their wedding night hotel, he makes sure their luggage is in the trunk.
- Handle payment for the officiant.
- Get reimbursed for the above.
- Don't lose the ring(s).
- Don't hit on female members of the wedding party, at least not the married ones.
- Make a clever toast, especially flattering to the bride.

The ushers have to deal with their own formalwear. They can assist with the bachelor party and act as a moral conscience (notice I used the word "act"). They may be asked to escort guests to their seats for the ceremony and walk down the aisle. At the reception, it is nice if they dance with their assigned bridesmaid and always remember to smile for the camera.

Flower girl/ring bearer

Both are optional in any wedding party. If you have a relative or close friend with a young child, it is wonderful to include them. Young girls seem to find this much more exciting than any boys I've come across. I guess some things never change. If need be, a girl can act as the ring bearer. Or you can just have flower girls.

Their prime responsibility is to *walk* down the aisle, either throwing petals or holding rings. Don't confuse the two. Recently my daughters, ages six and four, were in a wedding and they thought it was the most exciting thing in the world. We had just come back from a vacation and weren't able to make the rehearsal, but figured how hard can it be for them? Being of advanced intelligence and all. Well, while my oldest was walking down the aisle and throwing the petals, my little one started picking them up. Needless to say, it was totally adorable and got a big laugh from the audience. And therein lies the problem: These kids can steal the show. If you are totally obsessed with being the center of attention (and it is your unalienable right), you might skip the kids. If **39** you do include them, make sure at least one parent is around to control them and keep them happy and smiling, at least for the pictures. If the children are really shy, don't make them do this. It will just be one more thing to bring up in their shrink sessions later in life.

FUN FACTS

You must have a marriage license prior to your wedding day. Each state varies, but all of them have waiting periods, so you can't leave the license to that morning. There's only one exception to this rule. Any guesses? That's right, Nevada. That's how they keep all those twenty-four-hour wedding chapels thriving in Las Vegas.

Another tricky situation involves out-of-town attendants. This can become a mighty expensive proposition for them. If you or a relative or guest could put them up for a few days, rather than incurring the costs of a hotel, it would be a terrific help. Obviously, run this by your guest first to make sure she is comfortable with this arrangement. If this is not doable, prepare a list of local hotels, motels, and bed-and-breakfasts, with addresses, phone, and fax numbers. Provide her with this information well in advance. It will come in handy for other out-of-town guests as well. In fact, give a copy to your mom and his mom so they can provide it to their out-of-town friends and relatives. If you are having your reception at a hotel, check if there are special rates for your wedding party and guests. You can often get discounts on blocks of rooms, and they may even throw in a free honeymoon suite. It can be fun if you all stay together the night before, and some couples who get married in the morning or afternoon are thrilled to keep the party going into the night.

40   When you put together that list, get written confirmations of the costs. You don't want to find out, after the fact, that Aunt Doris spent twice as much as Cousin Flo. Or that they pulled a fast one on your guests. If you can reserve a block of rooms at a special group rate, they will provide reservations cards to include with the invitation. This is a great job for a mother who wants to be involved.

Overall, the defining role of the wedding party is not to provoke conflict. To support the bride and groom emotionally. And to have a great time at the wedding. In that way, they should behave no differently than each and every one of your guests.

6.

Training Your Fiancé

Congratulations, you've found the perfect man. Someone you want to share the rest of your life with. Well, you may as well start out on the right foot.

Many people will tell you to involve your fiancé in every step of planning this wedding. These are the same people who invented the vest with the simulated breasts so that men could "experience" nursing their babies. What planet are these people from?

Obviously there are exceptions to every rule, but I would estimate that 99 percent of prospective grooms don't want to hear about every aspect of this wedding, let alone be involved in it. Today men feel pressured to pretend they really care about this stuff. Do yourself a favor and give the guy a break. In the long run, you will be glad you did. This is not to say that men don't enjoy their wedding, but do you really think they care what color the tablecloths are? If you allow him to be uninvolved in all the mundane decisions, he may surprise you and rise to the occasion when you truly require his opinion.

Here's a little True or False quiz: Since many grooms (and brides) pay for all, or part of, their own weddings, they should be actively

41

42 involved in where the money goes. The correct answer is False. Ladies: Stop and think about the repercussions. Do you want him to know where you are spending your money for the rest of your lives? This is a very bad precedent, and an essential LIFE LESSON.

There are two ways to deal with a man who thinks he wants to be involved. Let him. That will teach him a lesson. Include him in every minuscule detail from the bridesmaids' stockings to the centerpieces. Have him examine different invitation samples and various calligraphy styles. Don't worry, he will crack in no time.

The other alternative is to put his boyish enthusiasm to good use before it wanes. Give him lists (you didn't expect him to start from scratch, did you?) of phone calls to be made and prices and other details to be confirmed. If he rises to the occasion, let him make the honeymoon arrangements, since that is the only part of this he really cares about. Obviously, he has to run everything by you, unless your idea of a perfect honeymoon is a baseball fantasy camp.

He can have opinions on the wedding and you can listen to them, filter out the garbage, and possibly come up with a good idea or two. It's much like dealing with your mother these days: Just practice nodding your head and acting receptive.

It's one thing to take his taste into account, it's another to let it dictate the affair. By all means have him look at potential reception sites, ask for his opinion on the food and the band. You don't want the pressure of making all these decisions autonomously. But let's be real. You don't want him any more involved than that. When your fiancé starts getting involved in picking out silverware patterns you know something is wrong.

My advice, as with a small child, is to give him two options—both of which you are comfortable with—and let him choose. That way he will think he had a say in the matter but, of course, you will have done all the legwork. *Welcome to marriage.*

Little boys don't spend countless hours fantasizing about their weddings. And this is not the time or place to discuss how they spend that time. Some advice experts think men should be totally involved in the "wedding experience." Make him involved, if he trivializes the wedding he's trivializing you, they spout. *Please* spare me this mumbo jumbo. You will have a much better sense of your relationship if you don't have unrealistic expectations of his involvement.

I can appreciate that the driving force of *his* money being spent could motivate a man to get involved. So bring him along when you register for the gifts. See what he thinks after spending a day looking at china patterns and crystal. He'll realize that this isn't as much fun as it's cracked up to be. At least for him. (Don't despair, there are registries that will spark even his interest; more later.)

The truth of the matter is that if men didn't feel pressured by women to feign interest or involvement, they would spend their entire engagement blissfully unaware of the surrounding chaos. As usual, it's our fault for having these expectations in the first place.

Look before you leap. If you really want his involvement you have to be willing to surrender control, to abide by his decisions, to accept his mother's involvement. Think about it: If you give him responsibility, who is he most likely to pawn it off on? And who has been dying to get her hands wet?

Remember your speech to your mother about how it's your wedding, not hers? Well, don't try this at home, but here's a little secret: It's really your wedding not his. Sure he's the essential ingredient, but his biggest concern is that it's not on Super Bowl Sunday. Granted, not all guys are like this, but most are. Because they are from Mars!

On the flip side you may be pleasantly surprised by all the things they can accomplish. From renting a tuxedo to planning a honeymoon. Just be careful to provide him with explicit directions. Explain everything before you let him go off on his own initiative. Think about this: Have you ever asked him to go grocery shopping without a list?

Since we are assuming that he is gainfully employed one could jump to the conclusion that if he can handle a job, he could handle a wedding. Well, we all know what happens when we assume.

44   I know you love this guy and want to give him the benefit of the doubt. Obviously he has good taste; he picked you. Just don't have unrealistic expectations of his interest in this wedding, and don't get frustrated by his lack of involvement. Think how annoying it would be if he actually had an opinion on everything.

7.

High Finance

With the cost of the average wedding hovering around the $20,000 mark, and in many cases soaring considerably higher, finances can become the most difficult aspect of the entire process.

Now is as good a time as any to remind you that your wedding is about the love you and your fiancé share, not about how fancy it will be. As with all the advice and information contained in this book, the most important thing to remember is to use common sense and keep your perspective. As the old saying goes, "Money can't buy happiness." Of course the second part is "unless you know where to shop." Later on, I'll show you some ways to shop to help have a dream wedding.

While there are no hard-and-fast rules, virtually everything you read on the subject divvies it up as follows:

BRIDE'S SIDE:
- reception
- photographer
- video
- music

46

- flowers
- liquor
- ceremony
- wedding dress
- invitations
- gratuities
- transportation
- wedding gift

GROOM'S SIDE:

- wedding gift

The groom's side has the *option* of covering the cost of a rehearsal dinner and may *elect* to pay for one or two items from column A, such as music or liquor.

Now you understand why her parents get the first call with the happy news. They have to start saving immediately. As a mother of two girls I find this startling and I would like to announce the formation of a national movement to split these costs equally. I figure if I start now, I could gain enough momentum in the next twenty years or so. It makes me wonder why we're spending so much time worrying about paying for college. At least there you can get student loans!

The reality is that most parents can't absorb the costs. Especially in New York City where, according to *The New York Times,* an average wedding costs $100,000! I personally don't find that news fit to print.

According to all the information on the subject, the average wedding is in the $17,000 to $20,000 range. (Don't yell at me, where do you think they get averages from?) This varies greatly depending on where you live. Obviously, big cities like New York, Los Angeles, or Chicago are going to cost more than someplace in South Dakota or Wyoming. It costs four times more in Los Angeles than in Montana, and more than five times more in New York City than in Kansas.

At the outset it's very difficult to figure out what the whole shebang will cost. Throughout the book I'll include money-saving tips, but it is up to you and your families to make some fundamental decisions first. **47** None is bigger than the guest list. The easiest way to save money is to cut the guest list. The largest piece of the wedding pie is the cost of the reception. That easily comprises 50 percent of your total budget. When you are hitting up your parents it helps to have some idea of the dollar figure involved. Ten thousand dollars may seem like a fortune, and it is, but not if you plan on getting married at the Plaza Hotel on a Saturday night.

If you have wealthy parents whose greatest pleasure is giving you the wedding of your dreams, no strings attached, then stop reading this chapter. Except for this last admonition: Even if they do have big bucks, do you really need to go crazy? Is it worth spending $100,000 on exotic flowers? If you have that much money, make a donation to charity in honor of your marriage.

For the rest of the world with limited financial resources or very long strings attached to the moola, read on.

Don't assume your parents owe it to you to pay for your entire wedding, and don't put them on the spot with that suggestion. I've heard of many folks who were more than willing to absorb the costs, until their spoiled brat of a daughter told them they had to.

It's difficult to know where to start. You need to pick a day and find a place for the reception and the ceremony. But you can't book a reception site until you know how many people you and your families are inviting. And you can't invite everybody unless you know you have the budget to do so. It's like a gigantic catch-22.

Start with the guest list, figure out how many people you guys want, then check with your parents and his. Have two lists: a) must haves and b) if we have the room. If you're not sure about someone, that automatically puts them on the second list.

Once you have an approximate guest list, look at some reception sites. Since this will be the largest expense and dictated by the size of your guest list you will start to have some idea of the expense involved. It's easy to suggest you make a list of the other major expenses and come up with an idea of how much money is involved, but it's not really

48   practical. There is a lot of time and work involved in this, and without knowing your budget it's kind of hard to put the cart before the horse.

You'll learn that the most expensive time to get married is a Saturday evening in June. So be flexible about the time and the month. It is much less expensive to get married in the afternoon and often much cheaper to get married on another night. If you've always wanted a summer wedding, look into Thursday or Friday evening. It's very easy for people to take a long weekend, especially in the summer. If you pick an off time to get married, not only will the reception be cheaper, but you will also save money on the band or DJ and the photographer and/or videographer. It's due to supply and demand. If they don't book a lot of parties on these evenings, it's money they weren't counting on and they can afford to give you a break.

Early on in this process you have to sit down and talk to your parents. See what they are comfortable contributing. They may have a nest egg saved just for this occasion. If you're the last of four daughters the well might be dry, but hopefully they've saved something for last. Don't make your sixty-five-year-old retired dad go back to work so you can have a black-tie affair.

Talk to his parents while you're at it. If he is more comfortable with doing this solo, that's fine. Especially if the groom's side has a guest list twice as long as the bride's, not to mention three times that of the "kids." (That's you, don't forget.) They should, in a literal sense, pay for the privilege.

Traditionally the groom's parents would absorb two major items in the wedding, i.e., the flowers and the liquor. But it's much easier if they are willing to commit to a dollar figure up front. It can't hurt to ask. It's not uncommon for those costs to escalate beyond the parents' expectations. They don't want to renege on their commitment, but they may have bitten off more than they can chew. Often they will want to know what the entire budget is, or, more specifically, what the bride's parents are shelling out.

The reality is that even with both sets of parents contributing, you and your fiancé will most likely be picking up part of the tab. You two should start saving as early as possible. Set up a separate checking account and try to put some money away each week. It's also a good place to deposit any engagement gifts that come your way. It's not a bad idea to keep this account solely for the wedding and write your checks out of it. Odds are you and your fiancé don't have a joint checking account yet, anyway.

If you will need to absorb the bulk of your wedding expenses, start economizing right now. Skip an evening out and put that money into your account. Rent a video instead of going out to the movies. Unexpected bonuses, income tax refunds (we can dream, can't we?), or payment from your insurance company (how's that for motivation to finally fill out those medical forms? and to not join an HMO)—not the money you live off—should go right into this checking account.

If you have extra money in the bank, earning 4 percent or less, maximize its potential. The simplest way is to invest that money in certificates of deposit (CDs) or mutual funds. CDs give you a higher interest rate, from 5 to 6 percent, but they require a minimum amount and you can't add money as you go along. Since the average engagement lasts twelve months, you can make some extra money and every little bit helps.

Mutual funds have higher rates and let you withdraw and deposit funds, but they require a larger initial deposit, around $2,000. Check out these options with your bank, your accountant, your dad—anybody who knows more than you and I do. Which in my case leaves a wide open field.

The best financial tip that I can offer and can relate to is *charge it.* Use your credit card for everything, and make sure your credit card is linked up with an airline to get mileage points or a new car, whatever. By the time you're done paying for this wedding you can fly halfway around the world without spending a dime. Or more to the point you may be able to get a free flight to your honeymoon destination. Not only that, this usually provides a built-in insurance policy through the credit card company. Remember that you'll eventually have to pay that credit card bill, so don't get too carried away and don't forget the enormous interest rates they charge if you don't pay your balance.

50   Once you figure out how much money you have to work with make up a pie chart. I could suggest spread sheets and all that mumbo jumbo, but all I'm trying to point out is your allocation. Figure out what is really important and where you want to spend your precious dollars. This will help when you start meeting with vendors, so you'll have an idea where you can splurge and where you should scrimp. Talk to your fiancé about how he thinks it should be spent.

Need I remind you that neither you nor your parents should go into debt for this wedding? Don't think that you have to have a fantasy affair in order to have a happy marriage. Quite the contrary.

Graciously accept what your parents offer. Truthfully they owe you nothing. They have fed, clothed, and educated you, and now you're on your own. How does it feel to be independent? So don't act like a spoiled brat and don't make them feel guilty. And, once more, don't equate money with love. It's an easy trap to fall into and one that can make this entire process unnecessarily painful and bitter.

You know your parents better than I do, but I'll bet that many of them will not give you money without expecting something in return. There are no free rides, so bear this fact in mind. It's not a bad idea to bring this up when you first discuss financial matters with dear old Mom and Dad. Tell them you love them, you appreciate this gift, and you a) welcome their advice, b) want to do this on your own, or, c) want them to butt out entirely. If you opt for (c), I would suggest waiting until the check clears. I'm half-kidding. The point is to understand your family dynamics and figure out the best way to handle it. The truth is you probably do want your mom's input . . . when *you* want it.

If you can learn to deal with dear old Mom, dealing with everything else should be a breeze. Here are some basic money-saving tips to keep in mind throughout your planning:

Negotiate:
Nothing is written in stone, it can't hurt to ask. If you can be flexible, so can they.

Get it in writing:

Always get written confirmation of costs and know exactly what you are buying. Make sure there are no extra costs or gratuities tacked on after the fact.

Substitute:

Yes, you can have the place of your dreams, but on Saturday afternoon instead of the evening.

Prioritize:

What is really important to you and where are you willing to sacrifice?

Avoid holidays:

Prices increase across the board. Everyone is busy during the holidays; remember supply and demand. Nowhere is it more obvious than with flowers, where prices can double or triple.

Don't pay retail:

From wedding gowns to invitations you can find discounted prices. From mail order to the Internet, there are ways to cut costs by 25 percent and more on certain items. If you do shop retail, wait until it goes on sale.

Beg, borrow, and steal:

Well, at least the first two. One friend may have a beautiful veil, another a time-share in the Bahamas. It can't hurt to ask.

Never mention money:

Or don't give them a price. Don't volunteer your budget until you hear a figure from them. Only let them know that their number is double yours *after* you've fainted.

52 **Comparison shop:**

But always compare oranges to oranges. A three-piece band is not the same as a ten-piece orchestra. Try to get at least three estimates, but not more than five. You need to get comparable values, not drive yourself crazy.

 Cut the guest list:

The simplest and most effective way to save money, though not the least painful.

8.

The "A" List

Composing the guest list is often an anxiety producing experience. You would like to share this day with everyone. And so would both your parents. Until they see how much it costs, that is. It's not going to happen for the vast majority of us, so you have to make some hard choices. Adding insult to injury, you have to make these choices way before the wedding date. The only way you can figure out how much everything is going to cost and where you can even have it is by determining the size of your wedding. It's a vicious circle.

You and your fiancé, as well as both sets of parents, have to make up two lists. Before you even begin, have some idea of what your parameters are. Do you want a small, family oriented wedding? Or a big bash? This will obviously have a great impact on your list. Back to the lists. There should be an "A" list, for the absolutes, and a "B" list for the borderlines. For the first go-round count the people on both lists: Maybe you're one of the lucky ones and it's a doable number for the wedding you want. Ha ha. Sorry, I didn't mean to laugh, but the odds of this happening are as good as you winning the lottery. Sure, it *could* happen.

Here's a more realistic dream. All the "A" list people combined

54 don't blow your budget. Take one more quick perusal of all the lists. If there are people on your parents' list that you never heard of, feel free to question them. There might be a logical explanation, but then again . . . The "A" list should be close relatives and close friends; that's it. This is one of the few times in your life that you will regret being part of a large close-knit family.

If you can't afford to invite everyone, you have some hard choices to make. The easiest is to ask his parents to cut theirs since they aren't paying. If they refuse, and money is at issue, perhaps they would like to contribute something extra to make up this difference? It's not fair to expect them to invite half your parents' list just because they aren't throwing this bash. But if they are way over I don't see any reason why they can't cover their costs, so to speak. The bottom line is that whomever is paying will feel that this buys them certain privileges. Which is true to a point. If I thought you could put both sets of parents in a room together and have them fight it out, I would. However, that's not going to work in most cases and it's up to you guys in most cases. Sorry to break the news. I told you this wasn't going to be easy.

Here's some help in cutting their lists, and that goes for your list, too:

- When was the last time you saw this person?
- When was the last time you spoke to this person?
- Did you send them a holiday card?

If the answers are a) I can't remember, b) you lost their telephone number, and c) you don't usually send Christmas cards, then cut them off your list. Then cross off anyone that is pure reciprocation. Just because you were invited to their daughter's wedding doesn't mean you have to return the favor. Is it really a favor? Would you have really cared if you weren't invited to that wedding? Be honest.

Conventional wisdom is that you shouldn't invite your office buddies, with the exception of your boss. I have a hard time with this. You see these people more than you see most people on this list, potentially more than you see your fiancé. You have been jabbering about this wedding at work. Truth be told, you've planned most of this wedding at work. Now you're supposed to cut all of them out? Maybe that's easier **55** for your parents, and maybe for him. But you have been sharing most of this with some of them. Look at it this way: If you quit tomorrow, would you stay in touch with anyone? Invite them. If you think it would cause tension to invite some but not others, then maybe it's better to skip them all. I just can't believe there aren't one or two people that aren't very dear to you. They might not be in your own department, but someone two floors away. Remember the one you eat lunch with every single day? Invite her, but tell her not to tell anyone, if that's the only way around it. Or confide in her, tell her your problem, and see what she suggests. I don't think you have to automatically invite your boss, especially if he or she is the only person invited from the office. Unless you have a relationship with him or her, don't do it just to suck up.

Here are some other considerations when cutting that list:

- Don't invite old friends you've lost contact with. If you have to go to a serious amount of trouble to find their address, that's a bad sign.
- Don't invite relatives you've never heard of before. How would they know and why should you care if they are insulted?
- Don't invite kids with the exception of nieces and nephews.
- Don't invite dates unless they are in a significant relationship. I know what it's like to be one of the few singles at a wedding, put at a table with some real losers. Tell them to think of it as another bad blind date.

Try not to have huge fights with your parents over this. Even if they are footing the bill, you should have certain veto privileges. If you've never heard of people on either parent's list, cut them. If you've never laid eyes on them, consider cutting. A word of caution before you cut on your parent's list: Hear them out first; they may have a good reason.

You will work this out. Because you have to. You may have to make some concessions about the location as well as some allowances throughout. When the going gets tough, bear in mind that very few, if any, weddings are called off due to unmanageable guest list problems.

56   Remember, you will get some rejections. As soon as you do, invite some of the people you had to delete on the first go-round. I won't tell them if you don't.

When you finally come up with a master list, type it out with full addresses. This can be used as your invitation list as well as for keeping a record of gifts and of your acknowledgments. It's one less thing to worry about down the road.

9.

Can't I Just Hire Someone?

In a perfect world, we would have someone do all the things we don't have time for, or can't be bothered with. For many years it was your mother. I hope that's no longer true. The good news is that there are people you can hire to do the bulk of your wedding planning. Wedding consultants can save you a lot of time, though there is some question whether or not they can save you money. The wedding planning profession is one of the fastest growing home based businesses, with sales of over $5 billion in 1997.

Since everything is about connections (another LIFE LESSON), nobody has more connections than a good wedding consultant. They can prod, plan, coordinate, avert potential disasters, and make the bride think this wedding stuff is a breeze. If they know what they are doing. There are training programs and certifications in this field. The Association of Bridal Consultants is the only organization dealing exclusively with wedding professionals. Ask for references and check them out. Interview them personally; as in any other profession, there will be ones you like and others that make your stomach turn. You will have to work closely with a wedding consultant so choose wisely. If she doesn't

58 have a sense of humor, move on—unless, of course, you don't have one either.

Their angle is that not only do they have connections, thereby reducing your stress and anxiety, they can also save you money. That is an arguable point. Their fee can be either an hourly rate, a flat fee, or a percentage of the total cost. You tell them your budget and they tell you what you can afford to do. However, I have spoken with some vendors, and they tell me that they jack up the prices when a wedding consultant is involved. I'm not sure if that is true or not.

If you have some extra money, I think this is a fabulous service. If you are on a tight budget, it doesn't really make sense. Don't undertake this service blindly. You need to familiarize yourself with all the particulars and have some idea of the costs involved, so you know if you are really getting a good deal. It makes sense that they have connections, and in a sense deal in bulk, resulting in better rates. Not to mention an encyclopedic knowledge of this industry. You could give yourself quite a headache trying to absorb everything.

It is vital that with your base of information you also share your personal desires (pertaining to the wedding, I mean). They are there to plan the wedding of *your* dreams, not theirs. Be honest about your expectations, about what is truly important to you, and if you don't have a strong opinion about something, listen to their advice. They don't have to plan all aspects. In fact, some people just hire them for their wedding day. That way they can deal with all the on-site headaches and help you relax. Since they didn't help plan the event they won't be at the top of their game, but for a price they will handle all the unforeseen emergencies.

This is better than an option that I'll discuss later, of having one of your attendants, or a relative, be in charge of the last-minute details. It's better to have someone who is not an invited guest be in charge of all the problems.

The primary task of a consultant is helping you allocate your resources. That's right; they will be like an accountant on your wedding budget. They will also keep you on schedule, telling you when it's time to do what. You just have to follow like a sheep, and believe me, I mean that in the best sense of the word. What could be better than your own personal wedding clock, beeping when it's time to get moving?

Don't ever let the consultant sign any contracts on your behalf. You should read and understand any agreements. Don't be under any obligation to use the vendors they suggest. You should have the absolute, final word on everything. Make certain they have ample time to plan your wedding and don't have a timing conflict with another affair that day.

FUN FACTS

Since ducks mate for life and symbolize fidelity, they are included in Japanese wedding processionals.

As I mentioned earlier, if you can't afford or don't want a wedding consultant to plan your entire wedding, look into hiring a professional for the day. What a relief it would be to have someone in charge, not to mention someone who can deal with the payments and gratuities. I've seen many weddings, including my own, where my dad and husband were off to the side writing checks. Listen, it's not the worst thing in the world, but it's one less thing to deal with. Hopefully, your wedding will go off without a glitch and you spent this money for nothing. It will still be the best money you've spent. They say you can't buy peace of mind, but this could come close.

10.

Eat, Drink, and Be Merry

It seems like just yesterday you weren't even engaged and you're already behind schedule in booking your ceremony and reception site(s). Talk about your quick turnaround time. How can you already be so late? It's sad, but true. If you want to get married in the foreseeable future, this must be done quickly. Especially if you're looking at prime wedding times, those being June or September on a Saturday night. Friday and Sunday nights are less expensive, and even less are the afternoon receptions. Booking a reception from November through early April will also save you some money.

Reception options are seemingly endless (as are the prices), from a local restaurant to a fancy hotel to your own backyard, anything goes. But not everything goes smoothly. First things first: You have to find a place to have the ceremony.

Many couples choose the house of worship in which the bride was raised. Overwhelmingly, weddings are held on the bride's home turf. If your family does not belong to a church you can always rent one for the occasion. You won't be given the first choice as would the members, but odds are they can squeeze you in. There are certain factors to consider:

- Do you like the officiant? The church may be gorgeous, but the priest may be a nightmare. Find out if he is part of the package or if you can bring in your own rabbi.
- Find out if there are other ceremonies being held that day. Could there be timing conflicts? It may not be another wedding, but if you're running late, the baby scheduled to be baptized next could be bawling his head off.
- Must you or can you provide your own decorations?

There is a lot more to a ceremony (in a later chapter); these are just the preliminaries so you can get up and running.

If the church or temple has a reception hall, you have just made your life a lot easier. Conversely, many receptions halls have a special area for the ceremony. This way you can have both in the same spot. One of the biggest problems with having the ceremony separate is the time and distance to the reception site. We've all been to weddings with a morning ceremony and had to cool our heels until the evening reception. There's never enough time to go home, change, and relax; but, magically, there is always too much time to kill. Are you supposed to go shopping in your fancy dress or maybe bowl a few frames? Of course, you're all starving by this time so you go to the diner and have no appetite for the actual reception. Consider your guests, especially the out-of-towners. If they rented a car, this will give them ample time to get lost. If they hitched a ride with other guests, they can spend the next several hours making small talk.

Check out the nondenominational chapels provided in most establishments. You can provide the officiant of your choice. Just make sure the chapel has adequate seating and decent acoustics. It's also much easier to utilize the flowers from the ceremony at the reception. Here's one more bonus point in my book: This way you can have the cocktail hour first, guests can arrive a little late, have time to relax, mingle, eat, and drink. They'll be in the perfect mood to enjoy the ceremony, instead of racing in late and having to go to the bathroom during the ceremony. Then they'll have time to get their appetites back for the reception. The only one missing the fun is you, but don't worry, all your girlfriends will come visit you. If you're hungry, you will be happily supplied with your own personal tray of hors d'oeuvres, not to mention drinks. That's what I did, and it got me relaxed and less nervous for the actual wedding. One last incentive: Nobody can throw rice or birdseed at you as you leave the chapel for the car.

Obviously you can have a beautiful church or synagogue wedding with the reception at another site. Just bear in mind the extra complications and transportation involved. It's worth consideration unless you want that traditional church or temple wedding. It costs money to use a house of worship and to hire an officiant. Hey, religion is big business. Be sure to include this cost in your budget, not to mention the transportation costs.

Look at potential sites for both so you can decide which way you want to go. Have a rough idea of the date and time you're looking for, but be flexible. You may go in wanting April, but feel lucky to come out with November. It is shocking how far in advance they book up. If you choose to have the ceremony separately, book it immediately. It doesn't matter where the reception is, because if the church is unavailable there isn't going to *be* one. You don't want to leave a deposit on a hall and find out your temple is booked that day. It's just one more headache to coordinate these two pieces of the puzzle.

It's recommended that for larger weddings, two hundred or more guests, book at least a year in advance; for smaller affairs, eight to twelve months prior. There are unlimited possibilities to choose from. Hotels, catering halls, galleries, private clubs, restaurants, resorts, homes, your home, parks, beaches, and even Dunkin' Donuts. Well, I don't know if they rent their space on a regular basis. On the Rosie O'Donnell show she featured newlyweds who had been married there. The bride was an employee of Dunkin' Donuts. Rosie was so charmed by this heartwarming story that her show picked up the tab for a honeymoon in Jamaica, and Dunkin' Donuts—probably thrilled with the free publicity—coughed up $5,000 as a wedding gift! There was no mention of what type of donuts were served to the guests. And we've all seen couples, hopefully not in person, getting married underwater, on roller coasters, and on top of mountains.

64   I am not, by any stretch of the imagination, advocating any of these more unusual spots. Feel free to be creative with certain limitations. At the risk of offending Mickey, I'm not a big fan of a Disney World wedding. Though they are unbelievably popular. Don't get me wrong, I love going there, but getting married there seems a bit goofy, if you ask me. Check around, get referrals—this is truly a word-of-mouth business. Don't just ask your friends. One of the best sources of information are other wedding vendors. After all, a photographer or DJ has seen more places then you ever will, hopefully. It's very telling to find out where they got married. Remember to ask them for referrals throughout the planning process. As with everything in life, don't take this as gospel; they may be in collusion. So check out every recommendation yourself.

If you've found the perfect place, only to learn it's booked for your day, make sure they have a deposit. Remember, money talks and if you pull out your checkbook it may guarantee you that spot. Feel free to have a momentary twinge of guilt about the other bride, but don't worry—you'll recover quickly.

Private catering can include everything from a boat to a golf course (not the miniature kind). Many catering companies will work with you to coordinate the entire wedding, and in a sense act as a contractor. They can also help pull many of the pieces together. They can arrange everything, including the tables, tableware, flowers, and favors. In a nutshell, they handle everything that has to do with the table.

Another decision to think about is sit-down versus buffet. It's a myth that buffet is cheaper; it can even wind up costing more. But it will usually mean a slightly shorter reception. Though you can save money if you go for a more ethnic buffet—try Italian, Mexican, or Chinese, or whatever. They lend themselves to a buffet style. It's usually less expensive than traditional wedding fare, and it's fun and different. Olé!

As I said earlier, traditionally the affair is held on the bride's turf. However, with everybody moving around and away from home, many couples opt to have it where they are currently living. Unless of course it's in a big city, where everything would cost twice as much as in the bride's quaint hometown.

So pick your location carefully. Set up parameters of how far you will travel. If you live in South Jersey don't expect everyone to drive three plus hours for a wedding in Connecticut. Try to stay within a reasonable distance. Again, there are obvious exceptions. If your family has a summer house on Martha's Vineyard, your guests can make it into a long weekend. Provided there are places for them to stay. You can't invite people, expect them to travel a long way, and not help them find overnight accommodations. Use common sense and put yourself in your guests' place.

Make appointments to look at potential sites. You can always drop by for a cursory look, to see if you are even interested in coming back. They say you can't judge a book by its cover, but if a place looks ratty on the outside, how great can it be on the inside? There are many important things to look for and questions to ask, but my main concern is if the place is run like a factory. By this I mean are numerous affairs held simultaneously? Back-to-back, so there is no margin of error to run over? Will you have exclusive access to the bridal room for the entire affair? I've heard of brides getting kicked out in the middle, because there was another bride waiting in the wings. Believe me, it happens.

I have heard many horror stories of parties running over their allotted time, and other guests inviting themselves to your cocktail hour. If possible find a place where this potential problem doesn't exist. A well-run site should be able to keep things entirely separate. Make sure the person in charge of your reception is giving you their undivided attention.

Once you find the place, get every detail in writing. And don't figure that you can squeeze in an extra table. If they tell you they can seat 120, don't go inviting 150 people. If your numbers don't jive, move on to another place. Unless you are willing to cut your guest list, don't invite too many people, hoping 20 percent won't attend. You can get away with a negative response rate closer to 5 percent. Don't waste your time praying it doesn't rain so you can squeeze in those two extra tables on the terrace. Is this something you really want to gamble on? There will most likely be enough unforeseen occurrences that you don't need to create your own problems.

66   Ask if you can see the room during an actual reception, for a party approximately your size. Bear in mind that if you do visit during an affair, dress the part. Don't intrude wearing T-shirts and jeans. I'm not suggesting you rent a tuxedo, but think how you would feel as hosts of a party if this happened to you. As uninvited guests you should be as unobtrusive as possible.

Always check that the site is fully licensed and insured. Feel free to ask to see the certificates. If they have nothing to hide they should be happy to oblige. Ask for a tasting before you choose a menu. Many places provide this service free, others charge a fee. But, it's better to pay now than to really pay later.

Here are some of the basic questions:

- Are you free on _____? (If you've picked a date or have your heart set on a particular time, this should be your first question. If the answer is no, the rest is moot.)
- What is the fee and exactly what does it cover? Are tax and gratuities included?
- What is the minimum and maximum attendance? Most places require a minimum guarantee.
- Are there other weddings running simultaneously?
- How many hours does this cover? What are the overtime fees?
- Are there discounts for off times?
- Can you provide the caterer, must I choose in-house services, or is there a list of alternatives?
- Where exactly will the cocktail hour and reception be held?
- Do you decorate these rooms in any way?
- Are there outside facilities (weather permitting) for photos, guests, and cocktails?
- What are the deposit and refund terms? (If you cancel and they rebook that date, your cancellation fee should be minimal.)
- Is there valet parking? What is the cost?
- Is there a coat check? What is the cost?

- Is there a separate room for the bride and groom to use?

- Do you provide colored linens? Is there an additional charge?
- What are the open bar options? Price difference for premium brands? Charge by the bottle or consumption?
- How many bartenders on duty?
- Do you provide the cake? Am I allowed to bring my own?
- Any restrictions on music?
- Do you provide centerpieces?
- Can you change the lighting?
- Can I see the actual decor of the rooms we will be using?
- Can I see the actual table settings from glasses to silverware? Can I get replacements?
- What type of meals do you offer vegetarians or kosher?
- Is smoking allowed? If not, and I would like an area set aside, can you accommodate that?
- Who will be running the party? Can I meet with them in person to review everything?
- Where will the gift table be, and do you provide security for it?
- Is the room air-conditioned? (It may not matter when you're looking in November, but for a July wedding???)
- Do you provide a rest room attendant? Is there an extra cost? (You should bring along a basket of toiletries for the ladies room, from hair spray to mints to brushes and safety pins, and a whole lot more.)
- When must I provide the final guest count?

Ask tons of questions and get all details, no matter how minute, in writing. Have a signed contract before you give them any money beyond a nonrefundable deposit to hold the space. Visit the site just one more time before you commit, to make sure it's everything you remembered. After a while it all blurs together.

If you are renting a space, but must provide all your services, you can save money. Not time and definitely not headaches. Many catering companies help with some or all of the services. The larger the wedding

68 the cheaper the price per person becomes. But don't delude yourself into thinking you'll save money by inviting fifty more guests. It doesn't work that way. Here are some additional questions if you are going this route:

- What is the server/guest ratio?
- Are the servers in-house or hired per party? Are there any requirements for the waiters? (I know when I was in college I waitressed an outside wedding with virtually no experience or training. I'm not saying you need a college degree—since we know that's not worth all that much—but it would be comforting to know that the servers were given some form of basic training.)
- What is the servers' attire?
- Does the caterer have liability insurance?
- Where and how is the food prepared? Is there a full kitchen on-site?
- Do you provide bartending services? How do you handle nonalcoholic drinks?

Obviously, many of the earlier set of questions are pertinent here and should be asked as well. Find out if they are associated with a trade organization, like the American Rental Association or the International Special Events Society, or check with the Better Business Bureau.

Everything under the sun is available for rent. Money can buy (almost) everything. You could have your reception in the wonderful land of Oz, if you were so inclined. But, don't get carried away. Remember your actual needs.

- Is the inventory state-of-the-art?
- Are they flexible about last minute changes? Extra place settings for your jerk cousin who brought along a date?
- References available?
- Will they clean up immediately and remove everything? If not, are you liable for anything? Make sure everything is returned on time or you will incur late fees.

In all cases, make real price comparisons; compare oranges to oranges. Or in this case, chicken to chicken. Filet mignon versus

Cornish hen can make a significant price difference per person. By the **69** way, I've heard some experts claim that fish never goes over that well and you should think twice before you offer that as a main course. If you're having children at the reception, ask if they have a special menu of things the rugrats will actually eat, like burgers, hot dogs, french fries. You get the idea; something fried and greasy and not all that nutritious. Not only might they actually eat their food, it should cost you less.

Try not to be too vague. Have some idea in mind of what you are looking for. I realize you don't know exactly what you want, but you can't go shopping without a grocery list. How can you expect a reasonable response to your query about a sit-down dinner, or maybe buffet, in the afternoon or evening, with approximately 125 to 175 people with an unusual menu? Would you be surprised to get extremely different responses? Would you be surprised to hear a dial tone?

When selecting any menu be careful of all the little extras that get snuck in; they can really add up. Sure you can have soup and salad. Why not have additional desserts, besides the wedding cake. Three choices of entrée, no problem. I expect whoever you are dealing with to be very accommodating, but everything has a price.

Ask to see a sampling of table linens. Your idea of pale pink may not match theirs, or the color may totally clash with your bridesmaids' dresses. Also, check out their table settings. Some are hideous and in some cases they may have substitutions available, if you ask. The same goes with centerpieces. They won't automatically volunteer this information, but many sites will provide candelabra or some viable alternative to costly flowers.

There are many different types of receptions, from morning brunches to black tie dinners. One of your foremost considerations is if you want a formal or informal approach. Here are some basic formats to consider.

 Cocktail reception:
You can have a three-hour informal reception without assigned seating (one less massive headache). This is less

formal and less expensive, and usually held in the late afternoon, so there is still time for your guests to go out to dinner—but if you do this right they shouldn't have to. You can still have a bar, hors d'oeuvres, tables, music, and dancing. In fact, the cocktail hour usually provides the best food of the entire affair. However, this won't make a traditional mother of the bride happy.

 Buffet:

If you want a more informal, relaxed party, this may be the way to go. Contrary to popular belief this does not necessarily save you money. What it will cut down on is the time. This type of reception is usually shorter. In fact it can be more expensive in the long run. Some places charge a per plate fee rather than a per person fee. And since you need waiters to clear the tables, you don't really save on the service side. Depending on your friends and family, the prospect of unlimited quantities can be way too much of an aphrodisiac. The downside is that many people—especially the older guests—want to be served and don't want to wait on endless lines. If you do go this route, you should still consider assigned seating so everyone doesn't crowd around one table, leaving one lonely couple at another.

 Sit-down:

The traditional, formal reception. The only thing you really lose here is the varied menu.

I've been to very few weddings where people left raving about the food. (I hope that's not a commentary on the caliber of affairs I'm invited to.) And when you spend the next day filling your friends in on the details, it's not usually about what you ate. Unless it was to complain about it, not to mention the small portions. Think about the weddings you've been to. As long as the liquor flowed and the music was playing, you probably don't remember the food, unless it was in a private restaurant where it was more a dinner than a party.

Many places have fabulous food, and so should your wedding, but a wedding is so much more than a meal. Of course, if the food really stinks, it can cast a pallor on the entire affair. If it's any consolation, you probably won't have a clue; you'll be too busy running around to actually taste anything. Which is why you should ask them to prepare a food basket for you. No matter what time you get married you will find yourselves in your hotel room starving. This could come in mighty handy.

Not to imply that your family and friends are lushes, but I think it is essential to have an open bar. A cash bar is way tacky. You don't invite your guests to a party and expect them to pay for part of it. If this expense is prohibitive, consider limiting it to wine and beer, or limit the hours of the open bar. Or during the cocktail hour have waiters serving wine and champagne. It's cheaper than hard liquor and if it is served to you it's hard to resist.

Always include a variety of nonalcoholic beverages as well. If you can't afford to serve any alcohol, have a reception earlier in the day. Definitely not in the evening. Even if you don't drink, you should respect the choice of your guests to imbibe, unless your religion forbids it. Just make sure they don't drive home.

There are three basic ways to go in the liquor department:

Consumption:
You pay only for what they consume, either by mixed drink or open bottles of wine and champagne. If this isn't a heavy drinking crowd, it may be your best bet.

Cocktail hour:
Only serve mixed drinks during this time. At the dinner only offer wine.

All inclusive:
If you have a group that likes to party, it may be best to get

one price for food and drink, and let them guzzle to their hearts' content. If you go this route make sure you aren't charged for those guests under the legal drinking age.

A few other considerations to bear in mind. When you are giving your final guest count, include meals for the musicians, photographer, your wedding consultant. Anyone that is not a traditional guest should still be allowed to eat. Some places make an alternative (read cheaper) meal, but that is your call. They still have to eat, but not in front of all the other guests. Let them have their privacy, it's difficult to balance a plate on the drums.

Depending on the type of reception you are holding, another option is to supply your own food. Since that task will fall to you and your mother, I would advise against it. Do you truly need or want this extra stress or aggravation? It may not be worth the money you save. I realize not everyone can afford a fancy, catered reception, but these days the options are limitless. You can even have your supermarket make up platters for your guests.

It is essential to feel comfortable with the reception manager or the caterer. You should either like or respect their style. Remember they are in charge and if they don't give you the impression of having their act together, they probably don't. They don't have to be your best friend, but if they are arrogant when you meet with them, and don't seem to respect your opinions, how do you think they'll be on your wedding day? *Worse* is the correct answer. Many things will reduce you to tears that day; this shouldn't be one of them. You'll be stressed out enough from your own family. You don't need it from the people you are paying (handsomely, I might add) to handle your reception.

Many couples choose theme weddings and their choice of foods reflects this. From a barbecue to a holiday theme the possibilities are endless. And, I feel, in most cases to be avoided. Remember this is a wedding, not a block party. It's wise not to get too exotic or too trendy. When in doubt err on the traditional side.

But if you must reflect a theme, the best place is with the cake. The cake can be the star attraction. Next to the bride that is. Give it a separate table and have it on display throughout the reception. It's common to use the bridesmaids' bouquets around it for decoration. Don't go overboard with the flavor. You can't please everyone all the time, but you can try with a basic flavor. How many people are going to want swiss almond, banana, cinnamon, mocha cake? One option is to have each layer a different flavor. That way you can't have guests complaining that they didn't get what they wanted. Well, at least there'll be fewer guests complaining.

Never decorate the cake with fresh flowers. Most have been sprayed with some form of pesticide and can be poisonous. Decorate it in other ways. The wedding cakes featured in magazines these days cost almost as much as the gowns, and are often more attractive. There are amazing options. The basic white cake with flowers is just one of them. Whether you choose a chocolate mousse cake, carrot cake, or cheesecake, make sure it's not too sweet.

Try different shapes, different textures, and different icings, or all three. You can have three layers, each a different shape, or a different color. It can be white, but that can be white chocolate. I don't consider myself a trendsetter, but when I got married back in 1985, I went for a vanilla cake with chocolate frosting. That was wild back then. I just know that I liked chocolate icing.

Remember the cake has a function beyond looking good. It is your dessert. So serve it first. You can then accompany it with fresh fruit or sorbet, but this is the main attraction. One way to cut costs is to have a small cake for display, but serve your guests from sheet cakes. If the reception site allows you to provide your own cake, check if they plan on charging you a "cutting fee."

The wedding cake was originally thrown at the bride, yet another fertility symbol. Jeez, you're barely married, and all they could think about was babies. As your mother taught you, it's not a good idea to throw food. Nor is it such a hot idea for the bride and groom to squish the cake in each other's face.

Let's recap the fundamentals. Begin as early as possible. Book your

74 ceremony site first, then your reception. Shop around and ask around. Compare apples to apples and get everything in writing. Have some idea of what you want, or at least what you don't want. Ask lots of questions and if you're not happy with the answers, or the tone of them, keep looking. Have your checkbook handy. If you're lucky enough to stumble upon the perfect place, book it. Many deposits are refundable and if they're not, the initial amount is usually insignificant in the scheme of things. Remember prices fluctuate greatly. Saturday evenings are always the most expensive and June weddings are still the most popular. Ask about discounts for alternative days and times. Check if there is a required, minimum guest count; many places have a hundred minimum and if you're up to eighty-six, you may as well invite some extras. Ask if you can donate leftover food to a homeless shelter. This is something you must organize in advance, but it could be a bonanza for the less fortunate and make you feel really good about helping others.

The perfect place may be right in your own backyard, literally. Bear in mind the amount of work, time, and coordination, not to mention chaos, involved in this. If you have a home grand enough to accommodate a large party, then odds are you can hire someone to plan the entire shebang, and you should. If it's in your house, it is in your face, literally and figuratively. If you choose an unusual site, take the temperature into account. Is there air conditioning or heat? Is there protection from the elements? If it rains is everyone hung out to dry? Is the ground level? Will the tables be on a slant? What about a dance floor? It's not easy dealing with the great outdoors.

Once you have decided upon the perfect place you can breath a big sigh of relief. While there is still tons of work to be done this will set everything in motion. You can now move on to all the other wedding vendors. Before you go, ask the reception manager if they have any recommendations, you may be pleasantly surprised.

This should be a swell party, so enjoy yourself. Remember not to leave in the middle. Don't book a flight for that evening. Stay, dance, and have fun until the very end. You will be glad you did.

11.

Say "Cheese"

Once you have a date and a place (not to mention a groom), the general consensus is that your next step is to hire a photographer.

Photography is arguably the most important part of a wedding. Long after this day is over your photographs will provide your lasting memories. Certainly you'll have your own vision of this day, which will gradually fade over time. While it's great to have a video, you won't be spending many Saturday nights plopped in front of your VCR with a bowl of popcorn watching this release.

However, you will be surprised at how often you glance at your album, at least initially. Later on, when you have kids, you will find that they are mesmerized by these pictures. I know mine are, I've had to hide the album because I was afraid of the damage they would cause. The only confusion is that they are not in any of the pictures. I hope the same is true for you first-time brides.

I believe this is one area where you shouldn't scrimp on the price. Not to say you shouldn't try to bargain or negotiate, just that this is one area not worth leaving to chance. This is also the most important service to get references about. Ask everyone who has gotten married in the last

76   ten years. Most of these guys (in the genderless sense) are established and will have been around a while. They should gladly supply references and you should check them all out, and even ask if you could see their finished album. Ask your newly married friends. All they want to do is show the pictures to anyone who expresses the slightest interest. Isn't it better to hear from someone you not only trust, but that you can ultimately blame if there are (God forbid) problems?

It's shocking how early everything books up and photographers are no exception. Most are booked nine months in advance, and many up to two years. So get your list of names and begin the search. Call and make appointments with a handful and visit their studios. If they will come to you, ask them to bring samples of entire albums. View these from beginning to end so you can get a sense of how they work. Don't just look at sample shots; any clown can get a few good pictures. You want to make sure they can capture your wedding day from start to finish.

If possible, choose someone familiar with your location. It's a great plus if they know the lay of the land before they even step foot in the place. On the other hand, a good professional should be able to scope out the place on a visit before the big day. Don't get someone who specializes in outdoor photography or children's shots. Get the guy who specializes in wedding photography. He's the one who will know a great shot and be prepared for it. Gently ask that he not be intrusive. Or share this story. "I was at a wedding and during the ceremony the photographer kept getting in the way. All the guests couldn't see. He blocked the video camera and the wedding party had to walk around him." Get assurances that nothing like that will happen at yours.

Talk to the photographer, think of him as the director of the picture. Needless to say you are the star. Establish some kind of rapport; if you can't, he's probably not the guy for you. Discuss your preferences with him. Do you want a more traditional approach with formal, posed shots? That's where the photographer tells you where and how to stand, when to smile, et cetera. Or are you more interested in the photojournalistic style that captures events as they occur, for a more candid effect? The correct answer is a combination of the two, and your photographer should utilize both styles.

Here are some questions to pose to your potential shutterbug:

- What is your style? Classic or candid? Directorial or bystander?
- Will you be the actual photographer? (Many large companies bait you with one and switch to another on your wedding day. Insist upon meeting with and seeing the samples of the real McCoy.)
- What type of packages do you offer? What is the cost of extra pix?
- Can we keep the negatives?
- When will we see the proofs?
- Can we have some assurance of the paper quality, so they don't fade or lose their color?
- Once we make our decision, when do we see the final product?
- Are you insured?
- Do you carry backup equipment, in case of mechanical failure?
- What is your payment schedule?
- What are your cancellation terms?
- What are your time constraints? Are you booked back-to-back? (You don't want them running late or running out in the middle.)
- What is your backup, in case you can't make the wedding? Will we get a partial reimbursement?

Once you've chosen a photographer, don't try to change his style or tell him how to do his job. Why did you hire him in the first place? Remember he is the professional. If you think he needs your advice, he can't be very good at his job. However, you can and should supply him with a list of essential photographs. You may be lucky enough to have several generations of family present at your wedding and would love to get a shot of the group. He won't know unless you tell him. Don't think you're going to remember to bring it up to him at the wedding. You'll be lucky if you remember your name. Your maiden one, that is.

78   Don't assume he is a mind reader. In my brother's wedding album we have a great family shot, but we forgot the bride; oops! So make specific lists of all the portraits you want. Obviously you can't do the same for candid shots, but you can ask that he focus on particular people at the reception. At the last couple of weddings I've attended they didn't take table photos; maybe this is the new passing phase. I hope it passes soon, because very often the table photos are the only shot you have of many of your guests. Appoint someone to assist the photographer, someone who knows who Aunt Bea is or can pick your godfather out of a crowd. You can supply him with a list, but if he can't put a face to the name, what good does it do?

You may be unpleasantly surprised by the cost of the pictures. Don't forget—in addition to your own blowup and albums, your parents and in-laws will undoubtedly want their own. Absolutely let them make their own selections. You don't need your choice of their pictures coming back to haunt you.

To give you some perspective, a good photographer will spend approximately thirty-five hours on your pictures, from the actual day to developing the pictures to preparing the album, not to mention meetings with you and other prospective clients. That's easily a week's worth of work. Remember, there are no second chances to capture your wedding. If worst comes to worst you can reshoot formal photographs of you and your groom, but that's about it.

I'm all for getting a bargain, but remember, "penny wise, pound foolish." It's not worth saving a few bucks if you're going to hate your pictures, or if you have to put up with a pushy, obnoxious photographer ruining your day.

Many of the experts think you should get to know your photographer prior to the wedding to build a relationship. While I advocate having a conversation about your hopes and dreams, I trust you are not transparent or shallow enough to think a relationship can evolve from an hour's discussion. The only good advice the experts have about "developing relationships" is that they don't suggest developing one with them. Don't ask someone with whom you actually have a relationship, like a friend or relative, to take the pictures. This is an awesome responsibility and unless one of them is a professional wedding photographer don't even consider it. It's one thing to take cute pictures at the beach, it's an entirely different matter to capture a wedding.

Here's where I am going to get on my soapbox and make what I think is a very important statement. You may instantly object, but please hear me out and promise to think about it. Promise? *Take your formal photographs before the ceremony.* Forget about it being bad luck for the groom to see the bride. It's worse luck to have your makeup already smeared. To keep your guests waiting an hour. To monopolize the best man for an hour while his date twiddles her thumbs. Okay, that's the least of our concerns. The best pictures are when you are freshest, when you are anticipating this moment. Get them out of the way. It will be such a relief to have it over with, you may actually be able to enjoy yourself. With all the other traditions going by the wayside I don't know why this superstition is still enforced.

The only other aspect I feel strongly about is to avoid the artsy-fartsy shots. I use that for lack of a better term. They are the dorky shots with your faces superimposed on the flowers. Your hands entwined over a champagne glass. You know what I mean. Don't pose for any shots that you are uncomfortable with. If you feel stupid, odds are you are going to look even stupider in the actual photo.

Once you've chosen your photographer, consider the following ideas and discuss them with him, beforehand:

- Shoot between the shots, i.e., before the wedding party is together, snap a photo with the bridesmaids putting on their finishing touches.
- Don't limit yourself to close-ups, go with some wide-angle shots.
- Vary the focus on shots—this helps isolate people within the picture.
- Use natural light whenever possible.
- Get candid shots on the dance floor.
- Use black-and-white throughout, for formal and candids. Be certain they don't use color film and print in b/w; the quality won't be as good.

80

- Try a story board—five or six pictures in sequence.
- Do something—don't just stand there beaming. Hug your friend, kneel down to your flower girl, and smell that bouquet. Use small gestures to bring these shots to life. If you're so happy you're crying, that can be a fabulous photo op.
- Stand up straight, don't slouch; keep your chin up, literally and figuratively.
- *Smile.*

Here are some pitfalls to avoid:

- Don't have formal portraits taken prior to your wedding day. Remember the old adage, all dressed up with no place to go. You may be dressed for the part, but it's not the same as how you look and feel on your actual wedding day.
- Don't use a family friend or rely on candid shots. Hire a professional.

In addition to the now popular trend of placing disposable cameras on each table, here's an interesting twist. Ask your guests who enjoy photography or always bring a camera to these events, to be responsible for one hour of the party. Provide them with a couple of rolls of film with a time frame listed and have them click away. This way everyone won't take the same shots and you'll get a slightly different perspective than the photographer's. Make sure they give you (or better yet, your mom) the rolls of film to be developed.

When you book the photographer, sign your contract with all the terms in writing, with firm prices that won't fluctuate next year. Be certain it includes the name of the actual photographer present at the event.

Most importantly leave enough time for the formal portraits of the wedding party and family—at least an hour. Here's a tip: Keep a small compact or blotter handy. Prolonged picture-taking can give you a shine you don't want. This is the simplest way to continue looking your best. Remember to keep your chin up, and smile, smile, smile.

12

Dress for Success

Drum roll please. Here's the moment you've all been waiting for. After all, next to the groom, what have we fantasized about all these years if not our wedding gown.

There is enough information on this particular subject to fill a book. But you and I have better things to do with our time. So here's the nitty gritty, and a little historical perspective.

Some people say the custom of wearing a white wedding dress started in 1840, when Queen Victoria wore an elegant white gown at her wedding. Prior to that, the bride just wore her favorite dress right out of her closet. Others claim the custom dates back to the early 1600's. In those days white represented affluence, virginity, and purity. If those are three words you wouldn't use to describe yourself, you are still eligible to wear white—or any other color for that matter. Though many people draw the line at black.

So let's start shopping for that perfect dress. It will be a long, strange trip. I know mine was. I went to the famed bridal building in Manhattan, with a friend who was getting married around the same time. We figured this would be a good way to get an overview of the

82 choices. We approached this day with much enthusiasm and anticipa-
tion, which quickly faded. When we told the saleswomen we were looking for something simple, without a long train or bells and whistles, they
practically sneered at us. You're lucky, since the current trend is toward
simple and elegant. Anyway, back to me. Instead of helping us, they
zoomed in on a young lady (I use that term loosely) who had brought
her mother, sisters, aunts, and I think a few cousins to shop with her.
She was trying on dresses that were so over the top and so wrong for her
body type that we even stopped to watch.

I tell you this for a few simple reasons, not simply because I like to
make fun of people. The first being that you shouldn't have to deal with
places that make you feel like dirt. You should have an iota of self-
awareness about what style suits you, and last but not least, you
shouldn't let them intimidate you. Or force you into something you
despise. But be flexible. Try on styles you never would have imagined.
A competent salesperson will have a good eye for what will work. It's
kind of fun, at least at first. But, don't assume salespeople speak the
gospel; the only thing they speak is commission. Try to deal with the
ones that don't seem to be constantly bullshitting you and saying you
look terrific in everything! The good ones will help you, they will find
styles that look good on you. They will listen when you speak.

That's why many women choose to deal with reputable, full-service
bridal salons. They can cost more, but they can also provide a certain
expertise and peace of mind. If you need some assistance, and truthfully
who doesn't, this may be the way to go. Especially if you don't have your
mom with you, and even if you do.

Which reminds me, don't shop alone. As mentioned earlier, don't
bring all your living female relatives, but find one or two persons whose
opinions you trust and respect. She (what are the odds it would be a
man?) would accompany you on your rounds to see all the options. It's
a good idea to have one constant, someone who has seen you in everything, from the sublime to the ridiculous. Most of your relatives, with
the possible exception of your mother, will think you look good in
everything. Friends can be more honest, or maybe they are just more

critical. Look at these women objectively and decide whose taste you like and most importantly who will speak the truth. This can be an overwhelming experience and since the dress can transform you into feeling like this isn't just a dream, you may find yourself getting carried away.

Whichever "lucky" gal comes along, it's not a bad idea for her to bring along a Polaroid camera. Take a picture of yourself in each gown and label it with the pertinent information, like name, style number, price, store, et cetera. After a while it all blurs together, and this will come in very handy.

Like everything else in life, this too is complicated. There is an entirely new vocabulary to learn so you can converse intelligently in weddinggownese. Here are the basics:

Styles

A-LINE: close at shoulders, flaring away to hem
PRINCESS: tight through the waist, then flares to hem
EMPIRE: high waistline, beginning at the bust
SHEATH: straight, body accentuating
BALL GOWN: full skirt, with tight bodice
BUSTLE: extra fabric in skirt, pulled together in back
TEA LENGTH: falls just inches above ankles

Then there are the necklines:
JEWEL: curves at base of neck
SWEETHEART: open, sweeping down to a heart shape
HALTER: wraps around the neck, baring the shoulders
PORTRAIT: off the shoulder, with a shawl-like appearance
COLLAR: high neck, often with lace or visible netting on top of the chest
BATEAU: straight across
DÉCOLLETAGE: low with cleavage
SCOOP: rounded and low, also showing some cleavage

84 Lengths

KNEE

TEA

ANKLE

FLOOR

Sleeves

CAP: short, fitted, just covering the shoulders

FITTED: tight on arm, varying in length

BALLOON: loose, elbow length

JULIET: short puff at shoulder, then fitted down length of the arm

T-SHIRT: straight, just like one

Fabrics

Fabrics include, but are not limited to: taffeta, linen, moire, charmeuse, shantung, faille, chintz, brocade, chiffon, organza, organdy, batiste, voile, jersey, silk, and satin.

I'm exhausted, I don't know about you. The other thing you should learn is that your body will now have a label. Are you:

- Full-figured
- Petite
- Tall
- Short-waisted
- Busty
- Pear-shaped .

Even if you always thought you fit at least four of these choices you will become a type. Certain styles will be recommended for your type. This is not a science, but certain types work better with certain styles. Basically you can't go wrong with the princess or A-line. The bride, or any woman for that matter, should accentuate the positive. If you're short or heavy, the A-line is elongating. If you have great boobs, play them up. Nothing distracts from flaws more than a little cleavage, except a lot of cleavage. Remember this is a wedding, not a nightclub.

Now that we're chugging along, let's move on to the train (get it?). You can have a train the same length as your gown, long enough to stretch down the aisle, or anywhere in between. The only other choice here is if you want it detachable or not. Some women only want to wear it for the ceremony, but don't want to deal with it at the reception. Detachable is the way to go, and it can usually be removed by simply unbuttoning it from the dress. If it is attached, you will have to bustle your train so it's not dragging along during the reception.

Wherever you shop, bring along a folder of the clippings you've ripped out of magazines. This will give the salespeople a good idea of what you think you want. Always note the issue and page number for easy reference. Anything can be tracked down that way. They may also have something similar or even exactly like the picture.

Back to the stores. You will learn that certain bridal salons are considered "authorized dealers" for certain manufacturers. Granted you're not buying a new car, but this can be important. Certain shops, some discount, some dishonest, may not deal directly with the manufacturer of your dress, though they will assure you that this will not pose any problems. That's probably true. But if you do have a problem with the dress, from a defect to a late delivery, you will not be able to deal directly with the manufacturer.

Some dress lines are exclusive to certain stores. Other shops will assure you that they can provide you with the exact dress you want. Just put down a deposit and they will order it for you. Don't assume that is true. Unless you see a sample or they can get one in, don't put any money down. What may occur is that they will order a similar dress and by the time it arrives you will have no recourse, as your wedding is right around the corner.

Which brings me to another important point. Tell them you need the dress by a date that is at least two to three months before your actual wedding date. Many salons can't guarantee delivery four months prior to the big day. The only problem this may pose is in alterations. Once the dress does arrive, see if they can hold it till the last weeks before the wedding. A lot of brides-to-be have some serious weight fluctuation as D Day approaches. It couldn't be the stress, could it?

Don't go crazy and think you have to go to every store in a hundred-mile radius of your house. Most stores have some overlap and you will just get dizzy, trying to see everything. Make an appointment for the bridal salons so you can get personal attention. Give a price range, but be flexible. Even if your budget is $1,500, what's wrong with trying on a sample dress for $250?

You can get lucky if you're a sample size. They can save you a small fortune. Bear in mind that they may require you to pay for additional alterations, so be sure to include that in the price. Even if the dress could use a dry-cleaning this could be the way to go. Speaking of cleaning, wear no or very little makeup. You don't want to leave lipstick stains on the gown.

Other options include:

WAREHOUSE SALES: They feature last year's models. Let me assure you that this is one fashion area that doesn't dramatically change year to year.

BUY DIRECT: Many manufacturers and designers deal directly with the public. Find the exact dress that you want, with all the relevant info. If it's from a magazine photo, note the exact issue and page number. Describing a long white dress with an empire waist isn't going to cut it. Always order a size larger. Whoever sizes wedding gowns has a very perverse view of the female anatomy. You can always take it in, but you can't take it out.

OUTLETS: Check out the yellow pages to see if any companies have outlets nearby. For example, Neiman Marcus Last Call Outlet in Austin, Texas, has featured sample size gowns at 80 percent off. The added bonus is that while you're there you can squeeze in some regular shopping.

TRUNK SALES: This is a sampling of a designer's entire line. Most stores can't carry the full line, so if there is a designer you love this is the best way to see it all in one place. The designer or a company representative will attend and they can advise you personally and potentially customize a gown for you. They often work with veils and headpieces as well.

VINTAGE SHOPS: They can have buried treasures at very reasonable prices.

Everyone has sales, from the local stores to the famous Vera Wang. For one-stop shopping, in the New York City area, there's always Kleinfeld's in Brooklyn. People fly in to shop in what is arguably *the* premier bridal store in the country. And big can mean bargains.

To quote Marcy Syms, "an educated consumer is our best customer." Especially a bride, if you know what you are looking for you can find it. If you know you can get it cheaper elsewhere, let the store know and I wouldn't be surprised if they became a bit more flexible. As my mother would say, "It doesn't hurt to ask."

Do you have your heart set on wearing dear old mom's dress? You're in luck if it's polyester, if you consider that lucky. It's the easiest fabric to restore; on the opposite spectrum is acetate. But don't try it at home. Take it to a professional, someone who specializes in restoring wedding gowns. Your chances are better if the fabric has kept its strength and shape, and proper storage is essential to achieve that.

However, proper storage isn't all that likely unless your mom got married in the last twenty years. Which reminds me to remind you not to forget to have your gown properly cleaned and packed afterward. Most dry cleaners provide this service, and most mothers provide storage space for the humongous box in your old closet.

Great, the dress is in fine shape. But now that you've taken a closer look it could use some updating. Again, deal with a pro. See if you can find a seamstress who specializes in this field. They can do magic, from a different neckline to additional beading. The possibilities are as endless as the price can be. Figure out if it's worth it to update the dress or pay a little more for a new one. It's your choice, just know what you're dealing with.

In all cases, allow yourself enough time for fittings; three are usually sufficient. The first is to get the measurements, the second to

88 double-check them. And the third, right before your wedding, is to allow for changes, either up or down, depending on how you are handling all this.

When going for alterations you should wear the undergarments you will wear on your wedding day. From the bra to pantyhose and a slip. Trust me. I forgot a slip and the night before my wedding borrowed one from my friend's sister. Did I mention she was a size four and I wasn't? It wasn't like I needed to breathe much, but there are some photos that look pretty tight around the waist. Not quite as tight as they would today. I probably couldn't get that slip over my thigh. Let's not go there.

FUN FACTS

It's here: America's first bridal superstore. Where else but New York? Based on a store in Paris, TATI is also a discount store. They claim to have everything, though not everything high end.

Most stores require a 50 percent deposit with the balance due on delivery. When you buy the dress, make sure there aren't hidden alteration costs. Be certain that the receipt has a very detailed description of your dress so there is no dispute when it actually arrives. If you're so organized that you have the dress six months in advance, well, that's your problem. Just kidding; we're just jealous.

Check if the store will hold it for you without charging you. If not, bring it home. Listen up everyone, this applies to you whenever you bring home your gown. Hang it, undisturbed, in a cool, dark, dry place. Put a clean white sheet over it. Not a garment bag or plastic from a dry cleaner. Check it out a week before your wedding date to see if it needs to be pressed at the cleaners. Don't go putting your iron on it.

There are other, less expensive options. You could borrow from a friend. If not the dress, maybe her headpiece if it matches your gown. There are rentals galore and a shocking amount of classified ads for not previously worn wedding gowns. You may be taking advantage of a broken heart, but look at the other perspective: She's just happy to be rid of it.

As with everything else, get all the details in writing before you pay a cent. In fact, pay for it with a credit card for two reasons: a) A federal consumer protection law covers all deposits made with credit cards. If there's a problem with the gown or the store goes bankrupt, you'll be covered. Figuratively speaking at least. b) You may as well get mileage points. By the time you're done with this wedding you'll be flying around the world.

Check out the store's cancellation policy. Not that you'll have to cancel your wedding, but in case you couldn't resist and kept looking. Odds are you'll lose your deposit. Don't forget to lie about your wedding date so you get the gown with time to spare.

The options are endless, as are the prices. So shop around, give yourself plenty of time so you don't have to settle or go way over budget. Though this is one of the hardest areas not to. Don't try on gowns way out of your price hemisphere because one could make you cry with happiness. When you get the bill it can make you cry without the happiness.

Keep an open mind, try on different styles. Focus on how it looks and feels on you, not in the magazine. Can you sit down, bend, dance? You're not looking to do push-ups in it, but you should be comfortable and able to breathe. Make sure it plays to your strengths and hides your flaws (if you have any). I know you will look beautiful in whatever you wear. I can't recall a bride who didn't.

13.

Pearls of Wisdom

You think the hard part's over? Well, we've only just begun.

Now you can begin to think about a headpiece and/or veil. Once you have the dress, you can dress it up, or not. It's simplest if you buy the accoutrements at the same place as the dress so you can see how everything looks together.

Historians claim the veil to be a strictly male invention, and one of the oldest devices to keep women subservient and hidden from other males. It is considered to be the one article of female attire that women did not create themselves. Though I have a hard time believing that some sadistic male didn't come up with pantyhose. The veil symbolizes virginity and modesty, and shields the bride from the evil eye (not to mention flashbulbs).

Since I'm assuming you don't usually wear veils, I suggest you try on everything. How else will you know what suits your head and your hair? Apparently custom-designed millinery is not that much more expensive, so if you don't see what you want perhaps you can order something.

As you may have guessed, the options are endless, from a simple

92 wreath of flowers to a tiara to a lace mantilla. Simple and elegant is always the best way to go. If you need a reminder, check out some wedding albums that are at least fifteen years old—when more was in. That will be a quick wake-up call.

Some religions require veils for the ceremony. Even if yours doesn't, I think it adds something. It's a beautiful moment when your dad lifts your veil, and kisses you for the last time as his little girl. And you know that even if you're forty years old and have been living away from home more than half your life, today you are his little girl.

The basic headpiece options include:

HEADBANDS: Not the elastic kind, but beautiful ornate styles with pearls, flowers, and pretty much anything you like.

RINGS: A round ring made of pearls or fresh (and silk) flowers.

CROWN: Your opportunity to truly feel like a princess. This sits full circle on your head.

TIARAS: A half crown, as it doesn't make a complete circle. Just as suitable for royalty, although not quite as ornate as the one Miss America parades around in. Even though a Miss Rhode Island purchased three for her wedding day, which rated a mention in *People.* One was for the ceremony, one for the reception, and one for her going-away outfit. I guess she developed a taste for them during her reign. Maybe that's what they mean when they say it's over the top.

VEILS: These are usually made of lace or tulle and can use the gown material as trim. They also vary in length:

Ballet: falls to the ankles

Chapel: falls two and one-third yards from the headpiece

Cathedral: falls three and one third yards

Blusher: over the face, often part of a longer veil

Bird Cage: falls below the chin

Fingertip: falls to your _____(fill in the blank)

Do you plan on wearing one for the ceremony? Be certain it works with the style of your gown. Regardless, you're not going to keep it on for the reception, are you? Most can be easily removed without affecting the headpiece. Some are attached with snaps, combs, or Velcro, others may be bustled and worn throughout the evening. In addition to bustling your train, make certain your maid of honor, or appointed person, learns how to do these both in advance. It's not something you want to be fooling around with during the reception. You may decide to remove the veil after the ceremony, but keep your headpiece on. In that case make certain that your headpiece stands alone. If you need to pin your headpiece on, use white bobby pins. It's better to match it rather than your hair.

If the glove fits wear it

This can be a stunning look for anyone, especially if your hands aren't your best feature or you can't stop biting your nails. If you're petite or have short arms, this probably isn't the way to go. Otherwise the dictating factor here is your sleeve length. If your gown is long sleeved you don't really need gloves. You can probably figure it out from there— the shorter the sleeve—the longer the glove. Once you hit sleeveless, try over-the-elbow gloves.

The big question is what do you do when it's time to slide the wedding ring on your finger. There are four options: a) Slit the seams on the ring finger prior to the ceremony, so you can just push the material down and then back up afterward. b) Remove your gloves at the altar and hand them to your maid of honor. Try doing this as unobtrusively as possible and don't bother trying to get them back on while you're up there. c) Have two pairs, one with the slit for the ceremony and another pair for the reception. If you plan on wearing them afterward, you're supposed to remove them when you're eating, at least for the cake. It's not just proper etiquette. Do you really want food stains all over them? d) Slide the ring over the glove as far as it will go, and deal with it later. Probably the easiest way to go.

Feet first

Here's the most important consideration in choosing wedding shoes: *comfort.* I know we are all willing to pay a certain price for beauty, but you really don't want to be in pain on your wedding day, and not be

94 able to dance, mingle, and enjoy yourself. I don't care how fabulous they are—put them back. I mean it. Right now.

Now that you're over that obsession you'll realize there is a wide array of choices. If you never wear heels, don't start now. That's all you need, to go walking down the aisle in shoes you can barely stand up in. Most shoes are dyeable, though I would steer clear of the dark colors. The dying process usually works the other way around.

Whatever you choose, try them with the dress. Break them in beforehand, prancing around your house, and don't forget to *scuff up the bottoms.* You don't want to be sliding down the aisle in your mint condition shoes.

I don't really see the need for a purse to go with those shoes. Sure you can spring for one, but when do you really plan on using it? Think you're going to need lipstick when you are walking down the aisle? It will never be big enough to be useful. There are lots of last-minute items you'll want to have with you, though not necessarily on you (more later, the list is large enough that you would need a garbage bag to carry everything around).

Pearls of wisdom

Pearls are clearly the accessory of choice. According to superstition, it's good luck to wear your grandmother's pearls (it's better luck if you get to keep them). A pearl necklace is often a popular engagement gift from the groom's parents or potentially from the groom himself. I borrowed my mother's.

The important part is to match your jewelry to your dress. I know I'm beating a dead horse here, but as you've probably deduced by now, your dress is the sun and everything else orbits around it. Obviously, if you have a high neckline the pearl necklace is out, but there's always earrings or a bracelet.

According to the Cultured Pearl Information Center in New York, 47 percent of all pearl sales in the United States are for weddings. (Where they get this information from is anyone's guess.) If diamonds are a girl's best friend, then pearls are a close second. Just as there are many types of diamonds there are hundreds of varieties of pearls. But guess what? You don't really need to know all that. Simply find a necklace that looks nice and is the right length. Odds are very good that there is someone in your family or a close friend that can lend you a strand.

Accessories can play an important role. Don't forget that they should only play a supporting role. The featured performance should be your wedding gown. The other accessory for you to think about and potentially for people to see is the garter. Even if you don't plan on exposing it to the crowd you may want to wear one. To fulfill the "something blue" if nothing else.

The ultimate accessory: your bridal party

There is no accessory that plays a larger role than the wedding party. A well-coordinated and beautifully attired bridal party is the ultimate accessory. It can also be the most difficult aspect of being in the wedding party. You know what? It doesn't have to be. There is a bright side, unlike the old days when there were a dozen girls wearing pink, frilly, hideous, gowns with matching hats. Check out some old wedding albums if you don't believe me. Today there are many more options. Of course, twenty years from now someone will probably laugh at what we think is the height of fashion. C'est la vie.

Today's bride (that means you) is much more understanding of this dilemma. Probably because she's been there, done that. Or she has taste, and values her relationships with these lucky gals. Whether or not your party ranges in size from Thumbelina to Dennis Rodman, there is a solution to your seemingly insurmountable obstacles.

First off, try to get everyone together for one shopping trip. Do this as early as possible, on the off chance you don't find something on the first go-round. Not to mention, the fifth, sixth, and seventh. You don't want to get so pressed for time that you wind up settling just to get this accomplished. This is the best way to get a sense of what everyone likes, what colors work, who looks good in what type of dress; you get the

96 idea. Make it fun, plan on going out to dinner and drinks afterward. This way you'll have something to look forward to. Though you may wish you had those drinks beforehand. Some experts say you should never bring the entire party with you the first time you head out. The rationale is that everyone will like something different. I suppose that could be true, but how are you supposed to know what that something is? Are you supposed to go back again and again, with one or two gals? That seems like a waste of time to me. This way you know everyone's preferences. A store that specializes in this area can help steer them in one direction. You can also see what looks good on which gal, though the final decision is up to you.

If your wedding party includes some out-of-town attendants, they don't have to fly in for this excursion. Tell them to get fitted at a local store, and to try some of the dresses you are favoring. Many attendants are not comfortable sharing their measurements. This way they can deal directly with the store and no one is the wiser. It is recommended that you order all the dresses together, since dye lots can vary. Make sure you ship her the dress beforehand to allow enough time for alterations.

I think you should start in a bridal store unless you only have one or two ladies in your wedding. If you have a larger party, this will give you a good initial overview, not to mention experienced help, used to dealing with large groups. They will be able to recommend certain styles and get accurate measurements. Bridal designers have gotten the message and have come up with some great stuff that can actually be worn again. That's the key: Almost everyone would rather pay more for a dress they actually like and can wear again.

You have many choices, and I'm not just talking about the style of the dress:

- The entire wedding party, including the MOH (maid or matron of honor), wears identical dresses.
- The entire wedding party, including the MOH, wears identical dresses in different colors.
- The entire wedding party, with the exception of the MOH, wears identical dresses, in the same or different colors.

- The entire wedding party wears the same color, but different style dresses.

Those are pretty much your options, as far as I can tell. The more diverse your party is, the more difficult it is to find a dress that works well on everyone. Some brides just tell them to pick any long dress as long as it's a certain color, and she doesn't even have veto power. Unless you want to accompany each and every gal, maybe you should trust them. Of course, everyone has one friend or relative that can't be trusted at least as far as their fashion sense goes. You may want to take a trip with her.

If you don't want floor-length gowns, that broadens the possibilities. Every department store has a wide selection that shows some leg. Many top designers have lines that are suitable for bridal parties, from Tahari to Nicole Miller. There is some fabulous stuff out there.

If you suspect that one of your attendants can't afford the dress (or she tells you point blank), what do you do? Offer to share the cost if you can or consider buying it as her gift for being in the wedding party. I know most brides are trying to cut costs, but if this will really help a dear friend, think about it. Many attendants are young and just starting out in the real world without great paying jobs. You may be in the same boat, but your parents are helping you out here. If you're not sure, talk to your mom if she's picking up the tab. She may be willing to absorb this cost. In the scheme of things it's not going to break the bank. Plenty of other stuff will. Ask the stores if you can get a price break for dealing in volume. If so, have both moms look for dresses there as well.

If you're having children in your wedding party, be prepared to find a wide array of dresses. They range from appalling to absolutely adorable. Not surprisingly, the price range goes from cheap to appalling. Again, the stores may be flexible on the price if you are buying more than one. Don't fall for the overpriced shoes. There are many discount shoe stores where you can find inexpensive dressy white shoes. Odds are pretty good that they won't be getting a lot of wear out of them anyway, so you don't have to buy top quality.

As far as shoes go for the rest of the attendants, give them a break. Let them pick what they want. If you say they can all wear black, they

98 can buy or may already have a pair of pumps that can be worn again and
again. Please don't insist they buy matching shoes, dyed to the exact
shade of fuschia as the dress. Do insist that they all get the same pantyhose. Even with floor-length gowns you'll see some ankle. You don't
want some sheer, some black, and some taupe, and that's easily avoid-
able. Pick up a few pairs just in case. If the dresses are dark, make certain the slip is also. In some photographs a lighter color slip may be
noticeable. Though I hope any dress you buy is lined, for the money
you're spending.

While this book is for you, the bride, you will have to deal with the
groom's attire, as well as that of his wedding party. No matter how much
you trust him, don't you want to see the tuxes or the suits that the boys
will be wearing? Technically they shouldn't wear tuxedos before six
o'clock. You know what? If he wants to wear one for an afternoon wedding, who cares what "they" say? "They" also claim that a formal
evening affair must include white tie and tails. Where is it written???

Go to a formalwear store and talk to them and see your options. For
morning or afternoon weddings men can wear an appropriately named
"morning suit." Though most guys will just refer to them all as monkey
suits. There is wide variety of choices—different lapels, single- and double-
breasted, and assorted styles of pants. Then there are the bow ties and
cummerbunds, not to mention shirts and vests. I guess the guys started
to get jealous that the women had so many choices, so they had to make
this almost as confusing. The big difference is that you're not going to
see that many different options, the more you shop around. Men can
also rent any or all accessories, including formal shoes. You should have
both fathers wear tuxes as well. You can probably rent one for the ring
bearer while you're at it. I've seen weddings where the men are in tuxes
and the ring bearer's in khakis. It doesn't really cut it. One last thing:
Make sure all the men try on their tuxedos before they leave the store,
in case additional alterations are needed. If you're renting a bunch of
tuxedos, they may even throw in the groom's as a bonus. It doesn't hurt
to ask.

Of course, the entire wedding party may decide to wear suits. There the array is endless. Sure it's more practical, you'll be able to wear it again. Though if you want matching styles, the initial cash outlay for all the men can be pretty hefty. If you go this way, try to coordinate the color of the groom's shirt to the wedding gown. He shouldn't wear white if your dress is ivory. The ties should be somewhat uniform and should reflect the color of the bridesmaids' dresses. You could always purchase them and make that your gift to the ushers.

With the exception of a very informal affair, don't let your fiancé get away with wearing just anything. I was at a wedding where the bride wore a beautiful floor-length dress. While it wasn't a traditional wedding dress in any sense, from the style to the color, it was nonetheless a stunning and formal choice. The groom on the other hand wasn't much of a dresser and she didn't want to push him. So he wore slacks and a sports coat and the best man wore a suit. On his wedding day, couldn't he at least go for a dark suit? Is that too much to ask? Is it any less comfortable to wear a sports coat than a suit jacket? And the contrast between the bride and groom only made it worse. I have a funny feeling that she regrets her choice, but it's too late for that, isn't it?

14.

To Video or Not to Video

When I got married in 1985, video hadn't really hit its stride. Plus we were trying to keep costs down (I now think of it as early research) and this was an easy thing for us to cut out. In those days it was not only very expensive, it was also very intrusive. The videographers were in your face and seemingly in the middle of everything; more specifically, the *lights* were, and they were blinding.

As the saying goes, we've come a long way, baby. While you could look at it as an extra expense, it can be a wonderful lasting memory. Obviously, you'll have your photographs, but give this serious consideration and try to work it into your budget. If you're having a small reception, perhaps a morning brunch, this isn't necessary. But if it's a swinging bash, this may be just the way to cover the action.

I'm personally not that fond of forcing your guests to wave to the camera and say something witty. Even the clever ones usually falter under this kind of pressure. I'm not quite sure why since we have come to expect this at almost every reception. Wouldn't you think we could find something intelligent to say? Unless of course your guests are already drunk; then you can't stop them from rambling on.

102   If you do decide to videotape, there are some different considerations in addition to those mentioned for the photographer.

- Go with a professional. Everyone thinks they know how to videotape, because they bought one when they had kids. The reality is that they could no more produce a quality tape than they could a three-tiered wedding cake.

- Ask your photographer for recommendations. It can't hurt to find someone he is comfortable working with, since they will be working closely together.

- Look at sample tapes and, as painful as this may be, watch them from beginning to end. (This may help you decide not to have one after all.) Look closely and stop making fun of everybody. Are the colors right? Can you hear the music and the toasts? Was it professionally edited? Is it choppy or is there a flow?

Once you find one you like, ask to see an additional tape and get references. It's almost always a good idea to hear what the bride has to say and if she was happy she did it (I don't mean getting married). While you're at it, ask her how often she has watched the tape. I don't mean to obsess about children, and if you don't plan on having any, you have my blessings. But you will never view your tape as much as when your kids discover it. For a brief period in their early years, you will dust it off and provide them with many hours of viewing pleasure. It may not be as educational as *Sesame Street,* but boy, will they get a kick out of it. I do believe I'm getting quite ahead of myself.

Back to reality. Some different questions to pose to a videographer are:

- Have they worked your ceremony and reception site before? If not, make certain they familiarize themselves with the lighting beforehand. If you are having a religious ceremony, check out any possible restrictions. Many people only video-tape the ceremony.

- Do they use multi-camera coverage during the ceremony?

- Do they provide portable lighting for the dance floor?

- What video format is used? The scale from lowest to highest quality is VHS, 8mm, Hi8, and SVHS.
- Are there extra charges? Overtime costs?
- Will they attend the rehearsal?
- Do they keep extra copies of the video on file? (In case yours is lost or damaged.)
- Who will actually be shooting the tape? Again, check out that person's work.
- How long will the tape run?
- Do they include collages? Computer generated graphics? Background music? Titles?
- Do they have backup equipment?

The "experts" will tell you to make sure that they have the latest technology, but how the heck are you supposed to know? My idea of high tech is the smallest camera around, but is that how the professionals operate?

Included in this contract should be how many copies of the videotape you will receive, and what type of format you are buying. Do you want a montage of pictures of you and your fiancé growing up? Getting ready for the wedding? A quick recap of the day to start off the tape? What type of music do you want as an accompaniment? A basic wedding video includes: titles, invitation, recap, ceremony, music, and graphics.

If you want to save money, don't use extra cameras at the reception. You don't even have to shoot the reception. Ask if there is a discount for additional purchases of the tape, though I can't imagine anyone except both sets of parents wanting them. Avoid special effects in the editing phase; the simpler the better and the cheaper.

Ask them to shoot on SVHS format and use HI-FI tape, which will give you better sound. As with your photographer, provide a list of must-have shots, especially if you want interviews with specific people, since they can't always get to everyone.

The popular types of videotapes are:

ROMANTIC: Includes lifestyle shots of the happy couple outside of the wedding day, often accompanied by their favorite songs.

104 **NOSTALGIC:** Childhood memories and snapshots.

DOCUMENTARY: Covers the entire day, from getting ready to collapsing from exhaustion; not the entire night.

STRAIGHT: No editing, you can get the tape at the end of the reception, warts and all.

ANIMATED: Like a photo insert with cutesy, identifying captions.

So decide if any of these appeal to you. If not, you can probably skip the video. If money is a major consideration, you should probably pass on this.

15.

High Anxiety

Feeling a tad stressed-out? Overwhelmed by everything that needs to be done and how much it's going to cost? Welcome to the club, you are now a full-fledged member.

One thing that you don't have to stress out about is the weather. Get this: Weatherdate Network, a meteorological consulting firm, promises it can deliver a long-range weather forecast with 75 percent accuracy up to a year in advance. (That's better odds than most marriages.) For $10 they will send you a printed report listing probable temperature, humidity, wind, precipitation, and sky cover for three-hour intervals all day. PS: Satisfaction is not guaranteed.

Stress is stress, but somehow it seems much more intense when you're trying to plan this (hopefully) once in a lifetime event. The biggest stress factor is to my mind the most obvious. No, it's not your mother or your fiancé—although they can come close. And no, it's not money, though that's right up there. It's *time.* There's never enough of it and it can, and will, continue to cause you the most anxiety. The time bind starts the minute you announce you're engaged. So when are you getting married? Have you picked a place? You just said yes and already

106 you're behind schedule, if you want to get married in the not so distant future.

Calm down, take a deep breath. Buy a notebook (you don't really need a fancy wedding planner) and start making lists. It's a great feeling to accomplish something and cross it off the list. Hopefully, this book will help you focus on what's important and what you need to do. Don't ever forget that many gals have walked down that aisle before you, and the great majority made it to the church on time.

There's another factor involved here, and while I'm not a scientist I would like to make a case for PWS. No, it's not a misprint. PMS is bad enough, but that doesn't last more than a week at a time. PWS stands for pre-wedding syndrome, and Midol is totally ineffective here.

Everything is up to you. Even if you hire a wedding consultant you need to look at everything and make all the decisions and keep your fiancé in the loop. Nobody wants to hear you complain, especially your intended. His likely response to your whining is to suggest eloping, not that it hasn't crossed your mind. While it may sound appealing at times, this is the moment you have always dreamt of. And besides, you wouldn't give him the satisfaction.

So take a deep breath, literally and figuratively, and relax. While you're at it, lie flat on your back, pull up your knees, close your eyes, inhale and exhale deeply. Repeat this until your breathing is slow and regular. You may as well take a quick snooze; you deserve it.

Though you can't always nap, sleep is one of the best ways to relieve stress. I know you're busy and there is not enough time in the day. Let something fall by the wayside. Skip *ER;* you can always tape it and watch later. You don't have to go out every weekend, sleep in. If it can't be restful, at least it could be fun.

Don't reach for that second cup of coffee. Caffeine, chocolate, and alcohol will unfailingly make you more stressed-out. Of course this may be a risk worth taking. At least you have some momentary pleasure and relief before you return to your cranky, agitated, PWS state.

While I don't want to make you sweat, consider exercising or yoga. Not only can it help you look better on your wedding day, it can make you feel better too. Isn't it about time you started believing that exercise **107** is good for you? Sweating cleanses you and makes you drink more water, which you should be doing anyway. Remember eight glasses a day?

It also can't hurt to treat yourself. Get a massage, a pedicure, or try aromatherapy. We can't all make it to a spa for a long weekend. Don't worry. There are plenty of things to do that won't cost a fortune and don't require a doctor's prescription.

Use common sense:
A month after your wedding you won't even remember the color of the tablecloths, so don't obsess over every detail.

Remember murphy's law:
No matter how much you worry, something will go wrong. Don't let it unhinge you and drive you crazy, just try to go with the flow.

Don't lose your perspective:
Yes, your wedding is important, but it is not the focus of the entire world. Life goes on, don't get too caught up in you.

Go to sleep:
That way you can dream about the way you want it to be.

Get organized:
Making checklists is stressful, but crossing each entry out, one by one, is bliss.

Delegate:
Ask your mom, his mom, your friends to help. In a pinch you can even ask your fiancé.

Win the lottery:
Short of that, try to stay relatively near your budget. Don't blow everything and plan something way beyond your means.

108

Eat well:
Don't go the fast-food route, try to eat three balanced meals. Don't take your frustrations out in a bowl of ice cream.

Step back:
Once you've gone through your initial round of planning, take a breather and enjoy your accomplishments. Try not to think about everything else at least for one day.

Kiss your boyfriend:
Remember what's really important here.

16.

Close to You

Music can make or break your reception. All evening affairs should have music, afternoons are optional, and if it's a morning brunch, just skip to the next chapter.

Many people consider this the most important ingredient of a successful party. How often do people talk about the band and dancing away the night, as opposed to the main course? Food for thought, isn't it?

It's not just spinning discs or strumming guitars; the DJ or bandleader is responsible for the flow of the show. A good one will set the tone right away. That's why it's vitally important to get a sense of their personality, or lack thereof. He will announce the newlyweds and hopefully get everybody up and dancing. He'll pause when food is being served, but get the action going again later.

Choosing a DJ or band is a matter of taste, not to mention budget. Odds are overwhelming that you will save lots of money going with a DJ. But many people can't imagine a wedding without a live band; it's more festive and flexible, in their view. When comparison shopping, look at the hourly fee rather than a flat fee.

110

BEATING A DEAD HORSE: Ask around for referrals, not just your friends. Try the photographer or the people at the catering hall. They've heard a lot more than you.

Always check them out for yourself, and when you meet with them, here are some questions to pose:

- Are they free on your wedding date?
- What is the cost? Prices vary dramatically. The more members of the band, the higher the price. The more bells and whistles and lights the DJ has, the higher the price.
- How often do they take breaks? Can a tape be played during these breaks?
- Do they provide a playlist of songs? That way you can delete and note your personal likes and dislikes. For some reason I get queasy when I hear "Celebration" and that's always played. Maybe that's why. Don't give them a list of every song you want played, but note the highlights. It will give them a good sense of your taste.
- Ask for a videotape. You can't see everyone in person, and this is a great way to see them in action.
- Have they performed at your wedding site? While this is not crucial, things can go much more smoothly if they know the lay of the land, not to mention its acoustics.
- Check out their repertoire. They should have a very wide range of songs or discs. If there are certain songs that you want that are a part of your ethnic or religious background, make that clear up front.
- Ask them for suggestions. They may have some great ideas on getting the party going without playing "Twist and Shout."

You want musicians that can motivate everyone to get up and dance. But you do have to trust them. While your eyes may roll back in your head at the thought of dancing "The Macarena," they know too well that this is the perfect way to get everyone up. It's shocking to see.

I personally could live without "YMCA," but again, the crowd gets into it. Unless you feel very strongly, let them play some of this dorky stuff. It appeals to all generations and especially people who might not be comfortable dancing otherwise.

Two of the most important factors are often overlooked. Be absolutely certain that there is ample space to fit the band or orchestra. It is all too common for the group to be larger than the space allocated. This will result in them spreading onto the dance floor or having to rearrange the tables. Neither is an appealing alternative. Make sure there is enough power for the group. Ask them what their needs are, don't assume the supply is adequate. While these problems can occur anywhere, they are more frequent in the less traditional reception sites and at home weddings.

If you hire a DJ, you want to be certain that he has a wide selection of tunes. Also, check out their lighting system. Many DJs provide additional lighting (at a cost), just be sure it's not too tacky or disco-like.

Unless you feel very strongly about a particular style, don't book a band that limits itself. Try to get a group that will appeal across the board. While you will never please all of your guests all of the time, you should make the effort. Don't you want them to have a good time? Let the bandleader know if you prefer instrumentals or vocals for specific songs, and in general.

As I've said before, make sure the band or DJ you pick is the one you get. If you really want particular members, list their names in the contract. Make sure you get the female lead singer that you heard, and not someone else. Many large companies pull people in by showing them their best, and then substituting the second tier. Again, if you go with the "A" group, you'll pay a premium. Another group may be perfectly fine; just make sure you view *their* performance before making your decision.

Many bands or DJs will invite you to come see them perform in person. They will have a set time when they invite prospective clients; don't expect to be invited to someone else's wedding. Take advantage of this opportunity. At the very least you'll meet other couples in your shoes, and you may even get a good idea from them. Not to mention that you'll find yourself in the company of women that are as, if not more, obsessed with talking about weddings.

When you do hear them, look for the following:

- Do you like the lead singer? Or do you like the vocals of the backup singer?
- Does one instrument monopolize the group or are they working in harmony?
- Is there a big gap between songs or is there a smooth transition?
- Does the bandleader lead too much? Or is he unobtrusive?
- Do they take creative liberties with songs? We've all heard groups playing our favorite tunes and we hardly recognize them.
- Do they take requests?
- What do they wear?
- Make sure you like the style and humor of the bandleader or DJ. If you don't feel a rapport you may regret it. It's not like he has to be your best friend, but you must feel comfortable with his performance. If you get the feeling that he is doing you a favor or not really listening to your requests, dump him. If they can't go to the trouble to accommodate you (within reason) for the money you are paying, then you don't need them.

When you are comparing prices, making your decision, and finally drawing up your contract, bear in mind:

- What time does the band set up? Preferably an hour before your guests' arrival.
- Are they booked back-to-back? If the timing is too close, don't risk it. Unless of course they are playing the wedding right before yours.
- Ask about specific timing—how many breaks, how long? Bands usually play forty-five minutes of each hour.
- Head count of musicians and specific names. If there are

changes beforehand you should have full approval or a money-back guarantee.

- Overtime fees? If the party is really rocking it may be worthwhile to keep it going.
- Additional fees? There shouldn't be administrative or union taxes on your bill. Gratuities are optional.
- Payment schedules. As with everything else, don't pay in full in advance.

Ask the band if they will provide music for your ceremony. One of them will probably provide this service for an additional fee. You don't need the entire group to serenade you down the aisle.

You and your fiancé might want to consider a ballroom dance class or two. It's fun, it's something you can do together, and you'll be able to do more than shuffle around for your first dance. Which brings us to that all-important decision. What song will it be?

Most couples don't have a special song, so glancing at the musician's list or asking around may be helpful. You should definitely pick one. One couple decided they didn't want any of the stereotypical wedding stuff, including the first dance. For some reason nobody told the master of ceremonies this and he announced their first dance as man and wife. The band didn't know what to do and choked. They played "Auld Lang Syne," and believe me it wasn't New Year's Eve. That's why it's so important for the bandleader and the manager or reception host to work closely with each other. They are jointly responsible for the flow of the entire party.

At any given time, there are popular favorites from "Color My World" to "Close to You" and "We've Only Just Begun." Celine Dion's "Because You Loved Me" is hot, and there are always the classics, like "Always and Forever" and "Our Love Is Here to Stay."

Whatever you pick, just make sure the band knows how to play your version or your DJ has the right CD. You don't want to hear anyone but Frank Sinatra singing "Fly Me to the Moon."

I've examined many lists of popular (and not so popular) first dance songs and I'm proud to say that mine isn't on any of them. There's nothing wrong with a little originality. Except in my case, it

114 involved me tracking down the sheet music. I've asked many women, and I've heard very few duplications. Every issue of every bride's magazine will list some compilation of first dance songs. As the mother of young children, I can't help but think of two of the most popular songs in a different light. Two Disney favorites are "Can You Feel the Love Tonight" and "A Whole New World." Both beautiful songs, but conjuring up images of *The Lion King* and *Aladdin,* doesn't strike me as particularly appropriate.

FUN FACTS

The money dance appears in various cultures, wherein the men pay for the privilege of dancing with the bride. The guests pin the money to her dress and cut in on each other after a few seconds. If you have to ask, you shouldn't be doing this at your wedding.

I was going to list some of the more popular songs, but that list is endless. Basically you can't go wrong with a classic. Almost anything from Johnny Mathis or Frank Sinatra is a safe bet, though I would steer clear of "That's Why the Lady Is a Tramp." Do listen to all the words first. You may be surprised by what you hear. And if there is a song that is special to you for any reason, go for it. Hey, it's your wedding.

Whether you choose a DJ or band, don't have them play at an ear-piercing decibel level. There is nothing more annoying than getting a headache from the music. Get everybody up and dancing, but when they sit down to eat let them hear each other. Not to mention hear yourself think.

17

A Rose by Any Other Name

This is arguably the easiest place to go way over budget. Flowers are beautiful, decorative, and amazingly expensive. Between the ceremony, reception, centerpieces, and bouquets, you could easily spend as much as an average wedding costs. I've read reports of society weddings proudly proclaiming that they spent $250,000 on the flowers alone.

You should begin looking at flowers at least three months before your date. If this is an area that you plan on going all out in, start six months before.

The most important piece of advice to follow is to pick flowers that are *in season.* You can get any type of flower year round, but the price may be exorbitant. If you have your heart set on a certain flower, a good florist can suggest a viable and less expensive alternative. Another trick of the trade is to go with a single type; that makes for a fuller bouquet with less flowers.

Talk to different florists and ask their advice. Explain your budget and see if they have any creative ideas to stretch your dollars. While flowers are beautiful they aren't always necessary. If your budget can't stretch to cover this area, there are ways to improvise.

116   One bride used the flowers from the rehearsal dinner as center-pieces. Granted, she had to add her own, but this dramatically cut her costs. The best part is that the groom's parents covered this, as part of the cost of the rehearsal dinner. If you donate your flowers to a nursing home or a hospital you may be able to write it off as a charitable deduction. Check with your accountant, or more to the point, have your parents check with theirs.

Another possibility is to amortize your ceremony flower costs. You can find out if there is another ceremony that day or weekend, and split the cost of the decoration. Or you can bring them along to the reception. I don't mean you personally. You have to have assign a responsible adult to this task.

You can use the bridesmaids' and your bouquets to decorate the cake table. I've heard of weddings where they just plunked them in a vase and used them as centerpieces. The truth is that the bridesmaids don't really need them during the reception.

If you wanted fresh flowers to decorate the pews at your ceremony, you may reconsider when you learn the cost. Try every three aisles or use ribbons or silk flowers instead.

No matter how you slice it, the bare minimum calls for bouquets for you and your wedding party (another incentive to keep it small). Boutonnieres for the men and corsages or nosegays for your moms and grandmoms. Many moms are willing to go without. Wrist corsages are clunky, they don't really want a pin in their new dress, and doesn't everyone know who they are?

The flowers are just a piece of the cost; a good chunk goes to labor. So another way to save money is to avoid elaborate arrangements. Some brides find independent florists that don't have the same overhead and are able to offer significant price reductions. Of course, you are then running the risk of not dealing with an established business.

The majority of you will find a local florist and proceed from there. Try to find someone who has wedding experience. Ask about delivery schedules; you don't want everything dropped off at the last minute.

Bring along swatches from the bridesmaids' gowns if you have them (leave them in your car or purse, so they're always handy) and you're worried that the flowers may clash. Do bring along pictures of flowers you love; who can ever remember their names? If you don't like something, tell the florist, don't make them guess. I know carnations are inexpensive and hearty, but I would rather carry dandelions.

It used to be that the traditional bride carried roses. This is no longer the case. Today anything goes. Considering the price of roses, this tradition was obviously started by a florist. There are beautiful arrangements of the same type flowers in different bold colors. Yet many brides still opt for an all-white bouquet and leave the color to the bridesmaids. They can each carry the same flower in different colors to great effect.

Before you select flowers for the ceremony, check if there are any restrictions. Find out how early the florist can arrive to set up that day. Make sure they have ample time to do your thing. You don't want to be waiting in the back while they are still decorating the pews.

Get all your estimates in writing so you can compare roses to roses. With luck, your florist will be familiar with your reception site and can advise you on additional decorations if need be. Or you can ask them to come along to get a glimpse of the place. Odds are you only need flowers for the centerpieces and, if you have a guest book, to decorate that table. As mentioned, you can use your bouquets for the cake table, or place petals around the surface.

Don't ever put fresh flowers on the cake itself. Almost all flowers have been sprayed with some type of pesticide that does nothing to enhance the flavor.

Many people are using flowering plants as centerpieces. They are often cheaper, last longer, and can even be replanted at the home of the lucky recipient. By the way, one clever way to choose the recipient is to give it to the person whose birthday is closest to this wedding day. I know many weddings where the guests practically come to blows over this, so you may be wise to come up with an idea on how to dispense the centerpieces to your guests. Otherwise people will be grabbing them off the table before the cake is even cut.

Flowers shouldn't overpower everything. Smaller bouquets and centerpieces are perfect. That way you can even see who is sitting across from you. A vase of mixed, wild flowers (not too wild) is beautiful and inexpensive for a less formal wedding. And what could be nicer than a bunch of tulips? I think it's nicer to have less of a beautiful flower than lots of a less attractive one (I won't name names). Remember: quality, not quantity.

Once you've chosen your flowers for the wedding party and the ceremony, you don't have to get them for the centerpieces. There are lots of other great ideas that will save you money.

Many reception halls have some sort of centerpieces if you ask. For some reason they are not quick to volunteer that information. Ranging from candelabras to silk flower arrangements, some can be hideous, but others can perfectly fit the bill. Just make sure your guests don't think they can take them home. Here are of some creative ideas you might want to consider:

- balloons
- fish bowls (your guests can bring home a pet)
- baskets
- hurricane lamps
- candles
- floating candles
- beautiful fruit
- picture frames with shots of the bride and groom as kids
- silk flowers (also available to rent)

Here's one of the more clever ideas I've heard: Instead of a large wedding cake, they used a miniature cake at each table. Not only did they have a beautiful centerpiece, but dessert was served. Bear in mind that it should be something that will hold up for a few hours, and look (and taste) good enough to eat.

A quick overview of the important points to bear in mind when flower shopping:

 Stay in season.

Stay with your colors:
Don't be too adventurous, make sure they don't clash with the wedding party or the reception hall decor.

Be consistent:
Don't pick a dozen different types of flowers.

Be natural:
Don't go for the more expensive, labor-intensive approach.

Stick with a style:
Don't have different looks for each bridesmaid (different dresses are sufficient) and be consistent with the centerpieces.

Double check
with your attendents that there are no allergy problems. That's all you need—to have them sneezing down the aisle.

Wear white:
When in doubt, use white for your bouquet. You can't go wrong with orchids or lily of the valley.

Pick your spots:
You can't (if you have a reasonable budget) decorate the entire church and reception. Pick focal points and concentrate your efforts.

Simple is better:
One stunning flower can complement, not compete with, your dress more than a large bouquet.

Don't forget to stop and smell the flowers:
While you're at it, bring some fresh flowers home or to the

office. Studies have indicated that this is a great pick-me-up. If you don't do it, who will?

During Victorian times, flowers conveyed a hidden meaning and lovers would send messages via bouquets. Carnations signify fascination and love, as do red chrysanthemums. Roses and tulips represent love. The ever popular lily of the valley means return of happiness and forget-me-nots stand for true love. I guess that's what they mean by the slogan "Say it with flowers."

18

You Are Hereby Invited

Here's the depressing part: You must finalize your guest list before you can deal with the invitations. If you skipped over that chapter because it was too overwhelming to deal with, I can't really blame you. But it's time to be strong and deal with the situation head-on.

When you order your invitations, the simplest mistake is to order by individuals, but most people are invited as couples. I assume your list is no different. So when you're counting, remember to count by invitation, not persons. Order another twenty-five while you're at it, for mistakes and extras. (Twenty-five is usually the minimum order.)

You should order approximately four to five months before the big day, since they should be mailed six to eight weeks before the main event. If you have a substantial "B" list and are hoping for rejections, start ten weeks before. With this time frame you have a safety net if the invitations don't arrive as ordered. If there are mistakes, you will have ample time to correct them, not to mention extra time to address them. As with all aspects of this planning process, your biggest problems arise when you're pressed for time.

122   The etiquette police have been fairly consistent on invitations. A standard one has fourteen lines of text and here are the basics:

- Names are spelled out fully, as are titles, such as Doctor. You don't list PhDs, but do include military titles.
- Dates and times are spelled out, as in the third of September, nineteen hundred and ninety-eight. I personally don't think you need to include "in the afternoon" after four o'clock, unless you often attend weddings in the middle of the night.
- Addresses and streets are written out, so try not to be friends with people who live on boulevards or in Indianapolis. If the street number hits triple digits or higher, it can be written numerically, i.e., 1600 Pennsylvania Avenue.
- British spelling style rules. It's "favour" and "honour" for a formal or religious ceremony; for civil, use "pleasure" of your company rather than "honour." And don't ask me why.
- Deceased parents should not be included, as they can't technically invite anybody to anything.
- If you can't agree on how to phrase the invitation due to divorce and remarriage, it is perfectly acceptable to only use the couple's names. Miss Lucy Eichner and Mr. Richard Mann, together with their families. . . . This can avert much potential conflict. Especially if you guys are footing the bill.
- Never have preprinted or computer printed envelopes; they should be handwritten.
- The invitation and all enclosures should be placed in the envelope facing out. They should be clearly visible when opening the envelope.
- Anyone over eighteen should receive their own invitation. If younger children are invited their names should be listed under the parents, in declining order of age.
- The inside envelope should not include first names, but read Mr. and Mrs. Max Eichner.

When you begin shopping around, you'll find that most of the hidden costs come with all the extras. Why should this be any different than everything else? You don't just need an invitation and an envelope to mail it in—you need all the trimmings. While that is arguable, the one thing it must include is a response card and stamped return envelope. If the reception is at a different place than the ceremony you need a reception card listing the time and address of the affair. Otherwise, the invitation states reception to follow. If you are on a tight budget you can list the reception details on the bottom of the invitation.

Extra money can be spent on envelope linings, and you can even have the directions printed on the same heavy paper stock. But think about it. Do you really save the envelopes? Doesn't your reception hall provide preprinted directions? The one extra definitely worth paying for is to have your return address printed on the mailing envelope. Who wants to go through the painstaking task of writing your address on each individual invitation? Even if you are hiring a calligrapher, it is much cheaper to go this route.

The invitation is your guests' first glimpse of your wedding and it should reflect that. If it is a formal, evening affair, then your invitation should be formal. If it's an outside party at your house, go with a more informal look, within reason. Your options are unlimited, but resist the flowers or the teddy bears. If you love that little girl look, get them on your checks (that's bad enough), not on your wedding invitations.

When you are looking at samples, don't forget that the cost is per invitation and you have to multiply that by X. It may sound reasonable at first, but this can quickly add up.

There are six standard types of invitations:

ENGRAVED: This is the most traditional, formal, and expensive.

THERMOGRAPHED: A less expensive alternative to engraved, it also has a raised, elegant look.

PRINTED: Not usually raised, but features a much larger selection of style and type.

CALLIGRAPHY: Handwritten invites, very time-consuming and expensive. Usually used for small, intimate weddings.

HAND-COLORED: Anything goes, your personal choice of color and design.

124   **BOX SET:** Preprinted, you fill in the blanks.

When you are shopping around, ask to see samples of all these types. This way you will know all your options. Also ask if they have some unusual samples of their work if nothing traditional strikes your fancy. Many stationers have thousands of designs to choose from. Again, don't make yourself crazy and think you have to see every potential invitation.

The biggest cost factor is the paper stock. So pick something substantial, but don't get carried away. Also, stay away from oversized invitations. Not only do they cost more, they require additional postage. Go with flat stock, nothing that has to be folded over. Not only will this double the postage, but who do you think does the folding?

When you're ordering, you will undoubtedly be asked if you would like coordinated thank-you notes. At first you may think it's a waste of money, but in the long run it can be cheaper and simpler than buying packaged cards.

What are announcement cards anyway? You may never have heard of them and there is no reason to start now. These are cards that aren't invitations, but merely announcements of your marriage. It's kind of like saying, I'm getting married, you're not invited, but send a gift anyway. If there are out-of-towners that you know won't attend, you can still send them an invitation. You also don't need printed cards for assigned seating in the chapel. And most reception halls provide place cards for the table.

A standard invitation should read as follows:

Mr. and Mrs. Max Eichner
request the honour of your presence
at the marriage of their daughter
Josie Sarah
to
Mr. Zachary Solomon
on Saturday, the seventh of May, nineteen hundred and ninety-eight
at half after seven o'clock in the evening
The Manor
Seventy-seven Fifth Avenue
New York, New York
Reception to follow

Normally the groom's parents are not mentioned. Since the bride's parents are hosting (paying) for the wedding they have this dubious honor. If your in-laws (almost) insist, explain this to them. If they persist, it's your call. I have no great advice, except not to ask their opinion in the first place, unless you are willing to follow it. If you ordered your invitations early, by the time this came up it would be too late.

If someone close to you (close enough to impose upon) has nice handwriting, beg them to address the envelopes. Splurge for a nice pen. If you can afford it, hire a professional calligrapher. Yes, it's an additional expense, but in the scheme of things, a minor one. Of course, this is how it all adds up.

Invitations are usually ordered in increments of twenty-five. That's why I suggested this number for extras. If you can get less and you don't have a "B" list, buy less. Don't forget to invite your wedding party; though you can skip the groom. Send invitations to your parents, it is a keepsake for them. For that matter, mail one to yourself. That way you can see the condition they arrive in and have some assurance your guests received them.

Don't just buy pretty stamps and assume the postage is adequate. Always take your completed, sealed, unstamped, invitations to the post office to be weighed. What could be more onerous than getting them all back, stamped with RETURNED FOR POSTAGE?

Remember, the basic money-saving tips are:
- Skip the envelope liners or just use it for the main envelope.
- Don't go for the engraved style.
- Don't get folded or oversized invitations.
- Skip the calligraphy.
- Skip the tissue paper. Originally it helped avoid smudging, but that's no longer the case.

Whoever addresses the invitations should have a clear, concise, typewritten (or computer printed) and up-to-date guest list. It can't hurt to address the thank-you notes at the same time. You'll thank me later, no need to send a note. It never hurts to double-check all the names and addresses against the master list. You can also use this list to keep a record of replies. But don't throw out your reply cards until after the wedding.

19.

Do Me a Favor

Do me a favor, save money and skip them. Do you really need to provide a cheap memento of this occasion? Unless you can afford to spring for something substantial don't bother. And even if you can afford it, why bother? I realize it started out as a way to thank your guests and provide them with a token of appreciation. However, I think the symbolism has become slightly distorted. Does a bag of Hershey's Kisses really convey your appreciation?

In the interest of fair play, I've provided a list of ideas if you are still so inclined. Basically it covers anything you can personalize with the name of the bride and groom, and usually the date of the wedding.

- wine bottles, with custom labels
- Hershey's Kisses and Hugs in tulle
- custom fortune cookies
- chocolate lollipops
- picture frames (can double as place card holders)
- instant lottery tickets
- bubbles
- candles

- magnets
- bud vases
- seed packets or bulbs
- potpourri
- bookmarks
- truffles
- chocolate
- chocolate name cards

This is certainly not an all-inclusive list. Besides a winning lottery ticket, is there anything here you really want? You can't go wrong with the traditional Jordanian almond candies as they symbolize health, wealth, happiness, fertility, and long life. That's why there are usually five in the package.

Can't you find a better way to spend your time and money? It takes endless hours to make something or even to buy something and then wrap it with personalized ribbons. If you still insist, the consensus is that we don't need another piece of junk. If there is something that has a meaningful connection to the couple, that's another story. One really nice idea is to make a donation to a charity in honor of your guests. Some couples provide gifts for the travelers and leave them discreetly in their hotel rooms. For the members of the wedding party, I've seen customized T-shirts, towels, and baseball caps. Bear in mind, this type of favor can cost a lot of money.

Other ideas include creating a tape of your favorite songs, including your wedding song. That takes some real thought and time and will certainly be used in your friends' cars, though I can't say the same for your parents' friends. Consider a local product. If the wedding is in Vermont, how about maple syrup? Another local idea that could obviously be translated for your area pertains to a Saturday night wedding. Upon their departure or placed in their cars by the valets, each guest receives a half-dozen bagels and *The New York Times.* Who wouldn't appreciate that?

One more thing: Don't bother spending money on personalized napkins and matches. Nobody should be smoking anyway; in fact they probably aren't even allowed to light up at your reception. Both are a big **129** waste of money.

One other twist that I think is the best of the bunch: We've all heard of disposable cameras, placed at each table, but here's a variation. As each guest or couple enters the reception, have a Polaroid taken. On their way out they can pick up the photo, tucked into a simple frame inscribed with the name of the bride and groom and the wedding date. They can be placed on a table or hung from a wedding tree, for the guests to pick up as they leave the reception. It's nice for your guests to have a picture of themselves all gussied up.

20.

Making Up Is Hard to Do

Naturally (or not so naturally), you want to look beautiful on your wedding day. More beautiful than usual. But you still want people to recognize you. As far as hair and makeup go, tread lightly. Don't go for any radical changes. This is another area that needs rehearsal.

Before we get started on makeup, there are some fundamental beauty tips that you can't buy at any cosmetic counter:

FACIALS: Start getting them a few months earlier, not right before the wedding. Your skin may initially be red and blotchy. A single facial won't make that dramatic a difference. If possible you should begin at least three months before. If your skin is healthy and clean it will take less makeup to hide those imperfections.

SMILE: Take a good look at your teeth; are they white or yellow? I'm not suggesting caps, and I don't know if those whitening toothpastes really work, but I do know something that does. Ask your dentist about bleaching your teeth. (At the very least get them cleaned right before your big day.) The bleaching process is really quite simple and painless. Your dentist will take an impression of your teeth and make a mold. You then put a prescribed formula in

132 it and wear this for a certain amount of hours, over a specified time period. You'll be pleasantly surprised by the results.

DRINK: Not alcohol, but water. One of the best beauty tips for your skin and overall health is to guzzle water. It's recommended you drink eight glasses a day.

SLEEP: Possibly the hardest thing to accomplish, especially when you have to constantly pee from all the water you're drinking. This can have the profoundest effect on your stressed-out body. You can't worry while you're sleeping, at least not consciously, and try not to grind your teeth. You don't want bags under your eyes in your wedding pictures, and you can't play catch-up the day before. Here are some tips for shut-eye. Many seem obvious, but we often ignore logic.

- Get on a schedule and stick to it.
- Exercise, but not too close to bedtime.
- Don't go to sleep hungry. Eat a full dinner so you won't snack all night.
- Kick caffeine—I personally consider this the last alternative, so just cut down.

WHITEN YOUR EYES: Professional photographers always use eye whitening drops, so try some out beforehand. A downside is that they may dilate your pupils and unfortunately, most don't work with contacts. By the way, make sure your contacts are clean. You might consider a new pair so there won't be any irritation. If you wear glasses, consider contacts. If you can't or won't, make sure your lenses are glare-proof and clean. I've heard of people borrowing an identical pair of frames without the lenses for the photo sessions.

Share these tips with your fiancé; they are all things men can do to look better. Especially since they can't cover up with makeup, which we all know can cover a myriad of problems and accentuate the positive. Even if you usually go au naturel you should wear some on your big day, if only for the simple reason that you will look better in the photographs. You'll appreciate it when you look at your wedding album.

Start with department store makeovers. They're accessible and usually free unless you get suckered into buying everything. Don't buy until you have done a fair sampling. Tell them it's for your wedding, and if it's during the day or night. Gratefully accept all the free samples. If you are happy with the results, ask if they make house calls and what they charge. Perhaps you can book them for your wedding day.

If you decide to use a professional makeup artist, ask around. Recent brides, photographers, your hairstylist might have recommendations. If you live near a big city, like Los Angeles or New York, you could call an agency that places professionals.

Try different looks and take a snapshot after each makeover. What looks good in person may not work for the camera, not that your Instamatic is the best judge, but it will give you an idea. Keep the makeup on for a few hours, roughly as long as the ceremony and reception would take, to see how it holds up. Do it before a night on the town. That way you won't be all made up with nowhere to go. When you go for makeovers, wear white or the color closest to your wedding dress, and if you plan on wearing that face out later, make sure you have a button-down shirt on so you don't smudge it when you change.

Many photographers strongly recommend using a professional makeup artist. Why not; it can only make them look better, not to mention you. Interestingly enough, they pretty much insist upon it if you're working with black-and-white photography.

If you do get a makeup artist to come to you, find out what it would cost to do the entire party, including the moms. This is a great extra treat for you to provide. Just let the artist know in advance so they come prepared. The added bonus in having them come to you is that they provide the makeup. As most of you know, the money you would spend at the makeup counter could almost make this cost effective.

If you decide to do your own makeup, or a friend offers their services, there are some basic tips:

DON'T OVERDO IT: Wear more than usual, but know when to say when.

USE FOUNDATION: Even if you don't normally. It gives a smooth, clean base and will help the makeup look better and last longer.

134 **USE MATTE SHADES:** These absorb rather than reflect the light.

ACCENTUATE YOUR EYES: Play up your eyes, including your eyebrows. Define them so they don't fade away.

CURL YOUR EYELASHES: Mascara isn't enough. This will make them look longer and your eyes look bigger.

BRUSH YOUR LIPS: When you're brushing your teeth, brush your lips. It exfoliates them. Use lipstick a shade or two darker than normal so it doesn't fade away in photos and don't forget lip liner and lip gloss.

VASELINE: Put a dab of Vaseline on your teeth to keep the lipstick off them.

USE WATERPROOF MASCARA: Between the lights and the emotions you'll be hotter than usual and you don't want this bleeding down your cheeks.

POWDER YOUR FACE. The biggest problem in photographs is a shiny face. So keep reapplying a light powder. Plant some on the groom's face too, if he'll let you.

DON'T PLAY THE MATCH GAME: Never match your eyeshadow to your eye color; this doesn't enhance them. And don't use frosted eyeshadow or lipstick.

Other problem spots for picture-taking include concealer. Go lightly with under-eye concealer, it can leave you looking like a raccoon. Also avoid brown- or yellow-based lipsticks if your teeth aren't pearly white.

Perfume comes under the category of not overdoing it. You don't want your guests to smell you before they see you walking down the aisle. Apply it lightly to the pressure points. Remember—the warmer the weather, the lighter the fragrance. Heat intensifies the smell, and it can also attract bugs.

Last, but not least. Put on your perfume before you put on that dress. This is one day you don't want to stain your clothes. The same goes for the makeup. Don't forget that button-down shirt, so you don't have to pull anything over your face or your hair.

21.

Hair Raising

Obviously the style of your hair will be dictated by your choice of a headpiece or the style of your dress. However, there are some basic guidelines:

- Meet with your stylist (or get one) prior to the wedding, and if possible bring along a picture of the dress and especially the headpiece. If you could bring the actual one, that would be even better.
- Bear in mind what type of wedding you are having. A black-tie evening calls for a more formal look than a Sunday brunch.
- Hair color looks best in the first two weeks. But don't wait until the last minute to chemically alter your hair in any way. A perm should be done a month before.
- If possible, have your hair done at the salon on your wedding day. This way everything is accessible and it's less expensive than a house call.
- Keep it off your face. It can look sloppy, but more importantly that wispy effect can create shadows on the pictures.

- If your hair is chemically treated, try to keep away from hot tubs, Jacuzzis, and chlorinated pools until the honeymoon. They can discolor your hair.
- Check out magazines for fabulous do's and bring the pictures to your hairdresser.

I know I said to look natural, and odds are you don't usually wear your hair in a chignon. But pulling your hair back can be a classy, elegant look and, just as important, easy to maintain. Not to mention working well with a headpiece. You might run this by your fiancé; some guys have strong opinions about their bride's hair. You know how they don't like it when you cut it short.

While you're at the hairdresser make an appointment with the manicurist. Your hands will be getting a tremendous amount of attention today. If you're a regular, keep it up. Just don't go for a real bright, garish color. Blue may be popular, but when you look back at your photos that may not be what you want to stand out. A perfect choice is a French manicure. The tips are very white and the rest of the nail is a softer white, beige, or pale pink.

If you still bite your nails or can't seem to grow them, think about getting a set of acrylic nails. Try them a few weeks before, and in all cases have your final manicure the day before, not the day of your wedding. It will still look good, but you won't have to worry about it on top of your normal bridal jitters.

If not now, when? If you're ever going to treat yourself or make yourself the best that you can be, it's on your wedding day.

22

Pump It Up

Forget about the church, today's bride wants to get to the gym on time. In a recent survey, *Bride's* magazine found that engaged women exercised at up to three times the rate of the average American. Let's face it, you're never going to get this kind of attention again. Unless you're competing in the Miss America pageant. In that case you can skip this chapter.

Dresses today leave little room for modesty and many brides believe if you've got it, flaunt it. I don't think you need to look like a stripper, but what's wrong with a sexy bride?

Listen, if you're ever going to get motivated to diet and/or exercise, it's now. You don't want to be sucking in your gut for the photographs all during your wedding day. So try to start at least six months before. As an added bonus it will help you relieve stress and may even be one of the rare moments in your day when you aren't obsessing about everything that needs to be done. You'll be too busy trying to catch your breath or dreaming about fattening food.

All the practical advice you've heard is still applicable. If you have any health problems talk to your doctor first. Get into a good cardiovascular

138 workout routine at least three times a week for an hour per session. Then you can begin to focus on your arms and stomach.

Walk everywhere, jog if you can. Park far away, take the stairs instead of the elevator. You've heard this all before. Don't forget, sex is a great calorie burner. See? This is one part you can share with your fiancé.

If you have the means, but not the mind, to get in shape, consider hiring a personal trainer. They can get you to do things you never thought humanly possible. If their bodies aren't incentive enough, then I don't know what is. Hopefully, they will get you going and you can take it from there.

Get motivated and stay motivated. It takes a while to see results, so start as early as possible and don't get discouraged. Don't fall into the trap that since you're working out you can eat everything. There are no free rides. If you must do something to excess, make it exercising, not eating. Another added benefit is that you'll drink more if you're sweating more, which is good for you and can fill you up.

I trust you're being feted at every turn, but try to resist the temptations. Cut down on the alcohol, there are a lot of empty calories there. You just have to decide what's worth it and what's not. I'm not suggesting you deprive yourself and make yourself miserable. If you're on a sensible diet, it's okay to splurge now and again. Just remember when you fall off that horse you have to get right back on.

Keep snacks handy when you're running around on all those wedding appointments. It's better to eat an apple than a candy bar. I know this is all logical, common sense. So what's your excuse? We all know it and we all (or most of us) don't want to deal with it. But on your wedding day, don't you want to look your best? And think how good you'll look on your honeymoon in that bikini.

23.

Registering for the Loot

Question: What should you do as soon as you're engaged, but no less than six months before your wedding day?

Answer: a) consider eloping

       b) win the lottery

       c) tell everyone to mind their own business

       d) register

I realize that is a trick question since technically the answer is (e) all of the above. However, the only one I can recommend in good conscience and can help you make happen is registering.

I know my first instinct was to register at Chase Manhattan Bank. I only wanted cash, I didn't need fancy china or silver. Well, thirteen years later I still don't have them and I only see the possibility of acquiring them becoming more and more remote. As your mother has often said, "You don't even know what you want." I hate to break it to you, but she may be right. But even if cash is the way you want to go, there are still engagement and shower gifts.

140   The wedding business is booming and one of the biggest by-products is the registry business. Companies finally wised up and today you can register for just about everything. Here are some of the highlights:

HONEYMOON REGISTRY: That's right. You make the plans, organize the details, and your guests contribute directly to an account set up by your travel agent or tour operator. (There may be a nominal fee.) How cool is this? Some places take it one step further, where you can pay for individual items, like a scuba diving lesson or a fancy dinner.

THE U.S. DEPARTMENT OF HOUSING AND URBAN DEVELOPMENT (HUD 1-800-225-5342) has a bridal registry mortgage account. It's available through banks and mortgage companies nationwide. Cash deposits are made into an interest-bearing account for a down payment on a house or apartment.

However, many people are not comfortable giving cash, even in these guises, and will want to purchase an actual gift. Well, the possibilities are seemingly endless. A recent survey of newlyweds found an 89 percent fulfilment rate of their registry choices. So be careful what you wish for. (Another LIFE LESSON.)

Nobody said it was going to be easy to get your man to register with you, but this is one area where he should come along for the ride. Or sign an affidavit that he will not bemoan your choices for the rest of your lives. If you want to start him off where he will be the most comfortable, that's not hard to do. Nowadays you can register everywhere. From Target, Home Depot, L.L. Bean, and Tower Records to Bed, Bath & Beyond, just to name a few.

It is suggested that you register in more than one place and that at least one is national. Try this on for size: There is a business called, simply enough, The Registry Shops. Based in Chicago with plans for national expansion, they display one of everything you could possibly want. They will deliver the whole kit and caboodle to the happy couple in one lump sum, where and when they want. I can just see a Mack truck backing up to your doorway.

If you go the conventional route, try not to register at more than three places; you'll have less overlap, and you don't want to look like pigs. Choose the ones you really want. If you register for the same item at different stores, you will have to continuously update your registries, instead of having the store do it for you.

Here are some basic guidelines:

- Register for a broad range of prices. Everyone works with a different budget and for the higher priced items people may opt to chip in.
- Check out special offers. Some places allow you to purchase the remaining items at a discount after your wedding date.
- Don't only use local stores. Get at least one national chain so guests from all over the country can have access.
- Ask lots of questions. What's the store's policy on returns, deliveries, and special orders?
- Loosen up. If something wild grabs you, put it on the list. It might tickle your guests' fancy as well.
- Involve your fiancé. If he starts to get glassy-eyed over the china patterns, move on to the electronic gadgets. That should perk him up.
- Register early. I know you have better things to do, but this can at least be fun.
- List your color motifs in various rooms on the registry.
- If you register for the same item in more than one place, remember to update all your lists.
- Don't forget to send thank-you notes; do it as soon as you get the gift.

Practically every store offers a registry service and luckily most are computerized. This way everything gets printed out and constantly updated. Many places have handheld computer gizmos, so you just flash on the code and bingo, you're registered.

The prices are not fixed; they are determined at the time of purchase. If you return something, it will go against the price paid. Most stores keep records up to a year after your wedding date, since technically you can give gifts during that entire year. It's also becoming increasingly easier to access registries via the Internet. Nobody has to even leave home to get their shopping done. Just point, click, punch in a credit card number, and have it shipped directly to the bride, gift-wrapped no less.

With all the great options, the only thing nobody has figured out is how to spread this information. It's considered way tacky to list it on any invitation, including the shower. It's kind of a telephone tag game. Make sure your family and wedding party know the particulars and share them with the world. Don't expect anyone to ask your fiancé and don't expect him to know the answer.

Rest assured, no matter how much stuff you register for, your Aunt Edna will still find some cheap, tacky gift. It goes without saying that you won't have a clue as to where to return it. Odds are it's probably left over from her wedding anyway.

24

Good Things Come
to Those Who Wait

Here's one part of the wedding process that is guaranteed to get your fiancé's attention: *the honeymoon.* After all, this is a big part of why he's putting up with the wedding in the first place. This is the only chapter of this book he may bother reading, not to mention getting involved in. It's one of the few areas that your mother may not have a strong opinion about. Your parents don't even want to think about you losing your virginity (haha).

The term honeymoon comes from the dark old days, when men would capture women against their will and hide out from one full moon to the next, roughly thirty days. During that time they would imbibe a daily drink containing honey, called mead. We have evolved since those days. We now drink margaritas and piña coladas. Unfortunately, we don't get a month off for the honeymoon.

Whatever amount of time you're able to take, make the most of it. But don't plan a nonstop, whirlwind trip. You don't want to come back from your honeymoon exhausted. This should be a time of rest and relaxation; you need it after that wedding.

144   There is an abundance of information about honeymoons. There is even a magazine called *Honeymoon.* Much of the material, from the so-called experts, suggests you and your fiancé write down your interests to see what you have in common, to better enable you to plan the perfect honeymoon. My theory is that if you don't know by now, maybe you should plan a longer engagement.

The real questions you should ask yourselves are:

- What's our budget? Look at it this way, you've spent so much on the wedding, what's a little bit more?
- How much time do we have? If you only have a week, do you want to spend two days of it traveling from here to there?
- Do you want to veg out or explore? Even if you're not a beach person this might be the perfect time to go to a warm weather resort, swim, and relax. Save the sightseeing tour for another vacation.
- Do you want to go to a "honeymoon spot"? Some places cater to honeymooners; do you want to be part of this group or just a regular couple? If you don't choose a honeymoon haven, let the hotel or resort know that you are on yours. There is always some freebie or upgrade that will be thrown your way.

The general consensus is that you should take it easy. Go somewhere just to relax rather than planning a tour of Europe. However, there is a case to be made for the fact that it may be a long time before you have the opportunity, time, and money for another big vacation. So go where you've always dreamed about, be it an African safari or Disney World. If you can't swing your dream location, make up for it with a luxurious hotel. Hopefully, you will be spending more time in it than usual. Don't blow all your money on airfare or you won't be able to afford anything when you get there.

There are many spots that combine the best of both worlds. We were only able to take a week for my honeymoon, which nixed my dream of Portugal. So we went to Kiawah Island. It sounds tropical, doesn't it? It's not in Hawaii, but South Carolina. You fly into Charleston and drive from there. This way we were on a beautiful resort and when we wanted to sightsee or dance the night away (alright, shop), we went back to Charleston. It may not be the most popular spot; that honor goes to Hawaii. I wonder where everyone from Hawaii goes?

Hawaii is followed by Jamaica, Mexico, Florida, Aruba, Tahiti, Cayman Islands, Bermuda, Greece, and the U.S. Virgin Islands, according to a survey by *Modern Bride* of thousands of travel agents. Spot a trend here?

Talk to a travel agent. Find out if there are any deals out there. They can also tell you if your destination is in season or not. You could get a fantastic deal, but it might be during tornado season. Do a little research to find out where there's gambling if you want more of a nightlife. Or golfing, if that's your fiancé's (I mean husband's) bag. Don't think you have to spend every minute together; you have the rest of your life. If you want to hang out at the beach while he's playing tennis—do it. You'll appreciate each other that much more when you meet up later.

When you decide on a place, make sure to book the reservations in your maiden name. I know you're anxious to be Mrs. Somebody, but you won't have any ID to prove it. Even if you're flying within the country you need a picture ID at every major airport to pass security. Do take along a copy of your marriage license in case you need proof for those special perks. Some airlines automatically upgrade honeymooners, so make sure they are informed in advance.

If you opt for a package deal, notify them that you want a king-size bed. Two double beds just won't cut it. There will be plenty of time for that later.

Many newlyweds suggest spending your wedding night and even the next night in a hotel. That way you're not running to catch an early flight, utterly exhausted. Don't have an evening wedding and plan to catch a six A.M. flight. Not only will you be bleary-eyed, but you won't have been able to open all your gifts and envelopes before you go. In many cases this can be a great indicator of what you can spend on your

146   honeymoon. Remember when I told you foreplay on your wedding night will consist of opening the envelopes?

Some couples, for financial or time constraints, don't go on a real honeymoon. A great substitution is to stay at home, turn off the phone and the alarm clocks, and relax. Eat out, take day trips, go to the movies, go to sleep, take long, hot bubble baths together. Do something you've always wanted to do. I don't know about you, but this sounds pretty good to me.

As usual there are some basic tips to save money:

BE FLEXIBLE: Your dream island may be too expensive, but the travel agent may have a perfect alternative.

TRAVEL OFF SEASON: Prices are much lower and places are less crowded. Just make sure it's not hurricane season.

CHARGE IT: Just like you did for all your wedding spending, keep it up. You get insurance and more mileage points this way. Consider burning the card when you get back.

RESEARCH: Don't go with the first deal that sounds good, there may be a better one right around the corner. Get on the phone, and on the Internet, and shop around.

DON'T FLY AWAY: There are undoubtedly some fabulous spots in your local area. So get in the car and drive.

No matter where you go, have your mail held at the post office, cancel your newspaper delivery, and have someone water the plants. Leave a copy of your itinerary with someone, but tell them not to call. Don't forget about your pets; make arrangements and have them in place before the wedding. In all the hoopla you don't want to forget about dropping Fido off at your sister's. Speaking of pets, a survey by the American Animal Hospital Association found that 6 percent of dog owners included their canine pals in either their wedding or honeymoon. Don't ask. Do you really want to know?

Have a great time and don't forget to send postcards.

25.

Destination Weddings

Combining the best of both worlds by having your honeymoon and wedding in the same spot, destination weddings are a growing trend. You pick a special place for your wedding and never leave, at least not for a week or two. It's like eloping except you bring along a small circle of friends and family. It's one way to keep the guest list small. The downside is they won't go home right after the wedding ends. Most people aren't flying in for the ceremony and jetting out the next day.

If you decide to go this route make sure to give your guests plenty of notice. The standard eight weeks isn't going to cut it here. They need to clear away vacation time, book a flight, dump the kids and the dog, and a million other assorted other details. Provide them with a list of the resorts in the area and all the pertinent info about this destination.

When you choose a site, either visit it personally or find a local wedding consultant to work with you. It's quite difficult to arrange everything over the phone without someone there to provide assistance. There are a lot of variables. I don't imagine that you could get married on just any beach, anywhere in the Caribbean. If you have a contact

148 there, they can find out for you. If you can't get there beforehand, consider the following:

> **HIRE A PROFESSIONAL:** There are wedding consultants everywhere and there are even professionals who specialize in destination markets.

> **GET A PACKAGE DEAL:** Some resorts have on-site services to help you arrange all the particulars, as do various wedding chapels. All you need to bring is a groom and a dress, and they take care of everything else. You may not love everything, but it's low maintenance and low stress on your part.

> **TRY A COMBINATION:** You can work with a local contact. While he or she may not be a professional wedding consultant, they can be your eyes and ears, and help with the legwork.

> **GET ORGANIZED:** No matter which option you choose, this is vital, even more so if you are pulling this together. You need to address a myriad of details, from airport transportation to shipping items in advance and confirming their arrival. Just don't send your wedding dress ahead or anything else that you can't live without. Be certain to pack it properly. Check with your salon or dressmaker or even your dry cleaner.

One of the highlights of a destination wedding is the location. You obviously picked it for a reason, be it a tropical paradise or a fabulous city like Paris. Either way, odds are you won't have to provide the entertainment for your guests, with the exception of your reception. Though it's not a bad idea to plan evenings with various people. One night for family, one with friends, and maybe a third with just your parents. With all these people around don't expect to spend every minute with your new husband.

You should only invite those people you truly believe will attend. Or those you truly believe will be insulted otherwise. You have the option of having a big party upon your return and inviting the troops. Of course one of the biggest selling points of a destination wedding is to avoid just that.

This is the one instance when you can send formal announcements of your marriage to the people you would have invited to a regular wed- **149** ding. This may, in the eyes of some, look like a thinly veiled plea for gifts, but don't let that stop you. The people who care about you will want to acknowledge your marriage, and the ones who don't, won't. It's as simple as that.

There will always be people, especially relatives, who will resent this newfangled idea of a wedding. Don't forget it's your wedding, not theirs. Do what's right for you.

26.

Standing on Ceremony

I am not going to resolve or address in any way any religious issues. You think I'm crazy enough to get mixed up in that? Suffice it to say that you will either a) marry someone of the same religion, or b) your parents will be so happy to get you married off that they won't complain. If the answer is c) none of the above, my prayers are with you—and that's as close to religion as I'm going to get.

Obviously your religious beliefs will dictate what type of ceremony is performed. Talk to your priest, pastor, minister, rabbi, or whatever. They will explain the details of the ceremony, including the vows you will be asked to recite. The bottom line is that your officiant will fill you in on all the details. If you have a mixed marriage (religion wise) you will have to find one or two clergymen (for lack of a better generic term) who will conduct a ceremony adapted to your situation. You can usually find someone who will accommodate your needs. The other option is to have a nonsectarian ceremony with a judge, mayor, or even the captain of The Love Boat. Just look for someone you like and respect.

Try to find someone who doesn't look at your guests as a captive audience or feel the need to share your entire family history with the

152   assemblage. Find out whether or not you must use the "in-house" clergyman, or you can substitute your own choice. You may love the chapel, but not the minister. Don't automatically assume that your family clergyman, or the "in-house" one, will automatically perform a ceremony tailored to you. Many religious representatives won't stray far from the path. Check this out if you want to personalize your wedding with your own vows.

Whatever you decide upon and whomever you decide to do it with, the best advice I can offer is to keep it short and simple. Nobody wants to sit through a long, tedious service. Obviously each religion has certain requirements, but there are ways to drag it out and others to keep up the pace. One of the easiest is regarding the vows. Endless love is one thing, endless vows are another. It's more difficult than you might imagine to express your sentiments in front of a crowd. You don't want to get too personal. If it's too gushy or maudlin it can make your guests uncomfortable. Make sure your focus is on commitment and love, and maintain a personal attitude throughout.

Be careful that you are in sync with your groom. It's one thing to surprise each other, it's another to go off on two totally divergent roads. Many couples modify the traditional vows. As you might imagine, most women don't want to promise to "obey." Isn't that perjury? If you really feel the need to express yourself, maybe your vows aren't the best place. They are certainly not the only place.

Choose certain hymns or music, or have a guest read a poem or psalm. If someone has a beautiful voice, they could perform at the ceremony. It's a wonderful way to honor a friend or relative. Another way to express yourself is to incorporate your heritage, which can be a beautiful and meaningful way to individualize and personalize this special time.

Discuss your thoughts with your officiant to see what he finds acceptable. Do what makes you happy, but don't do anything rash. This is a monumentous event, don't trivialize it.

Now that you have the actual ceremony worked out, you can deal with the particulars. Like the procession. If you want a white aisle runner, check with the church first; they may have one available. This is a symbol of God's holy ground. It shows that this is more than a marriage **153** of two people, but actively includes God's presence, much like a chuppah in a traditional Jewish ceremony. Oops, getting too close to religion again.

First things first. You have to seat your guests. Traditionally, Christian weddings have the bride's side on the left and the groom's on the right. It's just the opposite in a Jewish ceremony. This is a tradition I've never understood. The wedding symbolizes the uniting of two people and two families, so why can't they all just mix together? Like one big, happy family. The only rule there should be is that the immediate family occupy the first few rows. And the really tall people have to sit in the back. Make sure that the chairs in the first row aren't too close to the altar or stage. You need room for the wedding party and for a long train, and you don't need anybody breathing right down your back.

There is a beautiful tradition in the Jewish faith that can, and I think should, be incorporated into every wedding. The mother and father of both the bride and the groom escort their children, down the aisle. Both are giving away their babies, not just the father. What about dear old mom? What is she, chopped liver? She can give birth, but she can't give her little girl away? This way they are all active participants. In fact, they usually remain standing at the altar during the ceremony, which is certainly optional.

You can decide if you want your grandparents escorted down the aisle. If you are lucky enough to have their presence and they are healthy enough to do so, I think it is a lovely way of recognizing them. If you do they would be the first to proceed. If your parents don't accompany you both down the aisle then the mother of the groom is escorted down the aisle, with her husband following behind. The bride's mother is the last of the relatives down the aisle before the actual wedding party. Then the processional begins with the ushers according to height, followed by bridesmaids. Then the maid or matron of honor, the ring bearer, and the flower girl.

The guests rise, the music changes, and Here Comes the Bride, with her father or with both parents. They bring her to her groom, lift her veil, kiss her adieu, and the ceremony begins. This is the simplest

154   standard processional. Religions can dictate other versions and you can incorporate any changes you choose.

It is your choice if you wish the wedding party, but not the MOH or best man, to sit or remain standing during the ceremony. That's why you had the rehearsal. Nothing is ever simple, nor should you assume that anything is obvious. That's why it is important to follow your own religious guidelines. Talk to your clergyman and decide what works best for your needs. You don't have to be Jewish to have both parents walk you down the aisle, just flexible. Nothing is, or should be, carved in stone.

There is a wide range of music that can be played for the processional, so do a little research. You can go with the standards, but it doesn't have to be "Here Comes the Bride," unless that is what you want. The music can be played by an organist, a single musician on the harp, or even on tape. See what works for you and what you can afford.

The best man should have your ring and the MOH should have his. I think the ring bearer should be purely decorative. I'm not sure I would want a little boy responsible for the bands. You should immediately hand your bouquet to your maid of honor until the ceremony is over.

Try to relax up there. Don't attempt to resemble a mannequin. Don't lock your knees, and don't think you have to stand perfectly still. Traditionally, the bride stands to the left of the groom. This isn't by accident. In the olden days this enabled the groom to reach for his sword with his right hand if he needed it for defense. It is not traditional for the groom to carry a sword any longer. Make sure you both eat something beforehand so you're not lightheaded. Or should I say, more lightheaded than normal. Don't forget to take a bathroom break ahead of time. That would be pretty embarrassing. The entire ceremony happens *fast* and yours will be no exception. Everyone gets through it, and so will you.

When it's over you'll kiss your husband for the first time, as a married couple. No ceremony is complete without one, but don't make it a sloppy, wet one. A simple kiss is all the audience needs and wants to see. In Roman days the kiss signified the sealing of the marriage contract. The newlyweds will lead the processional back down the aisle, followed by the maid of honor and best man, a pair of bridesmaids and ushers, then the little performers (if any). The parents and close relatives in the first row are next, and usually the rows clear out from front to back.

Then it's on to the receiving line. This is totally optional, and not a bad idea. This way everyone can say congratulations and you don't have to obsess about conversing with them at the reception. Which is virtually impossible if you have a large wedding. The receiving line should include both sets of parents and the bride and groom. Some include the maid of honor, and others even throw in the best man. Entirely your call, though traditionally the best man is not present; I guess he is supposed to be outside tying cans and decorating the newlyweds' car. I've heard one clever twist on this theme. The bride and groom walked back up the aisle and made a receiving line at each pew, greeting each row of guests as they departed. Their parents waited outside to greet the guests.

Theme weddings can drastically alter your ceremony. My thinking is unless you are getting married on Halloween you shouldn't go there. It's bad enough to have the reception be a recreation of the star ship *Enterprise,* but does the ceremony have to be reminiscent of *Star Trek,* as well? Should your wedding vows include the phrase "Beam me up, Scotty"?

Lately I've been to weddings that featured programs listing all the members of the wedding party and the musical choices. Some include a favorite psalm or poem. Some are photocopied, others are elaborately engraved. Either way I think it's a waste of money. Hopefully your guests know who the bride and groom are; do they really need to know the ushers' names? Are the guests supposed to take it home and save it? Like a playbill? The next thing you know, advertising will be inserted to help offset the cost of a wedding. You laugh, but nothing would surprise me.

27.

Get Me to the Church on Time

So there you are, looking stunning I might add, in your wedding gown trying to hail a cab. With all the planning and all the details, one that can get lost in the shuffle is transportation. How do you and yours plan on getting to the ceremony and/or reception? What about when the party's over?

There are many options for getting to your wedding. Hailing a cab isn't your best one. Vehicles are truly important if you are getting married at a site other than your reception. In that case you should consider using three. One for the groom and best man and perhaps his parents, another for the bride and her parents and a third for her attendants. Usually the female members of the party are all together, either at her house or a hotel getting dolled up. That way they can all leave from the same location. One way to save is just to have the limousine for the bride and her parents to get to the church. Have everyone else get a ride there. Just make sure they have transportation to the reception, and that you reserve spaces near the entrance for the cars belonging to the wedding party. All they need is to be late because they couldn't find a place to park.

158   A great way to economize is to order a luxury car instead of a limo. You can probably get one for the entire day for less than what you'd pay for a few hours' rental for that limo. Just make sure you have a licensed driver (one that will remain sober) and make your reservations well in advance. They may even bring the car to your doorstep.

FUN FACTS

A judge in Kentucky sentenced a couple to a combined sentence of twenty-five years in prison and then married them. Not right away; it took the better part of an hour for them to obtain a marriage license and come up with makeshift rings. The article didn't mention anything about conjugal visits.

Check out your options. Look at any of these cars beforehand. Ask about less expensive choices. Don't blindly take the bridal package offered; it's not usually the most economical and often has extra touches that you might not need. Find out exactly what you are getting for your money. How is payment handled? Do you plan on asking the driver to make a quick pit stop at an ATM machine on the way to the reception? What about overtime costs and gratuities? Does it seat six or eight? You don't really want your bridesmaids sitting on each other's laps. Don't assume the car will be white; if that's what you want, tell them. Other companies deal with custom and vintage car rentals. It would be pretty cool to pull up in one of those, maybe even a Rolls Royce. Odds are that would be a unique experience.

There are, not surprisingly, lots more options. Some rather unconventional. You can rent a horse and carriage, which is a nice touch if you're going through Central Park, but it doesn't really work if you're using a highway. Winter weddings have a horse and sleigh. I've heard of everything—hot air balloons, fire engines, motorcycles, and jet skis. Do you really want to wear a wet suit on your wedding day? Is this a desperate cry for attention? Not to mention insurance?

If you are having your reception at an atypical place or at your home, consider potential traffic and parking problems. You may want to hire a valet service. Let the local police department know as they may want to make provisions for traffic control.

Don't forget to figure out how you are going to get from the reception to your hotel on your wedding night. Don't ask the best man, *at* the wedding, if he could do you a favor. Work this out beforehand and have the suitcases in the trunk before the wedding. If the groom drove to the wedding, what does he plan on doing with his car? It's best if someone brings him. He's probably so nervous, he's better off in the passenger seat.

If you have lots of out of-town-guests, and/or the ceremony and reception are nowhere near each other, consider renting a bus. Preferably not a school bus, but something a little nicer, perhaps air-conditioned or heated. It doesn't have to be glamorous, merely clean and reliable. It also has to make the return trip. That way your guests don't have to worry about driving at night or having a few drinks, at least until they get back to their own car. I don't think you could arrange for each individual drop off. Just because you're relaxing in the back of a limo with a bottle of champagne doesn't mean you should forget about the little people.

28.

The Wedding Band

When you were looking, thinking, and fantasizing about engagement rings, did you give any thought to wedding bands? Or were you so overwhelmed by diamonds that you couldn't think about anything else? Or maybe you bought both parts of a set, or picked out a complementing ring at the same time.

If you got this out of the way, then congratulations. Your prize is to skip ahead to the next chapter. Everyone else read on.

Before you look for a wedding band it is important to discuss this with your fiancé. Are we talking band or bands? Is it an issue whether or not he will wear one? Is it to you? Have this fight, I mean discussion, in private beforehand.

I am personally a strong advocate of the double ring ceremony. Unless he is in an occupation where it is a hazard to wear a ring then there is no excuse. The other possibility is that he absolutely abhors jewelry. There are men that won't even wear a watch, let alone a chain or a ring. It drives them crazy to have anything on their skin. However, the great majority don't fall into either category. They may not be used to wearing a ring, but they adjust. They can certainly become accustomed

162 to it over time. This is just the first and simplest of the many adjustments they'd better get used to.

They should realize that the band is a symbol of your marriage, a declaration of your love. A signal to every other woman that he's taken, keep your hands off. Hey, it's easier than wearing a sign.

I realize the big difference is that women want a ring. How do you think men would like it if you didn't want to wear one? I don't imagine that very many men would find this behavior socially acceptable. Talk about your equal rights. What's good for the goose is good for the gander. He's married, then he's wearing a wedding band. If you can't get him to agree at this stage in your relationship, it's going to be a bumpy ride.

Now that that's resolved, there are a few more decisions to be made. Do you plan on wearing your band with the engagement ring? Or moving it to your right ring finger? Did you pass on the engagement ring and this is the main attraction? Do you want a band that will match your husband's?

If you go for matching, keep it simple, nothing too feminine or fancy. You can have matching bands that are not exactly identical. His can be thicker, yours could always have diamonds. If he is still resistant, get him the plainest most unobtrusive band you can find.

You may have naively thought, "How many choices can there be?" Have you learned nothing about this marriage business? There are thousands of choices; they can make you dizzy. They can feature different textures, be intertwined, or woven. They can be antiques or facsimiles. They can have stones, diamonds, or facets. They can even spell out love. Anything goes.

Just remember what this signifies. For many centuries the band has been a symbol of love and faith. The reason it is worn on the ring finger is because it's called the ring finger. Just kidding. There are various theories in this regard. One was that the vein in this finger traveled to the heart, though this has been scientifically disproved. Another is based on the observation that this finger can't be extended straight out by itself. Try it; every other finger can point straight out solitarily, except for your ring finger. Thus the other fingers protect it and the ring.

Perhaps the most logical is that in the olden days, during a Christian ceremony, the priest arrived at this finger after counting from the thumb, "in the name of the Father, the Son, and the Holy Spirit." This corresponds to the Jewish ceremony, because there the ring is placed on the bride's right index finger, and she moves it after the ceremony.

Don't go too trendy or too crazy. After all, it is something you hope to be wearing for many years to come. That is, of course, until you trade up for that diamond anniversary band, but that's way down the road.

29.

Old, New, Borrowed, and Blue

"Something old, something new, something borrowed, something blue, and a silver sixpence in your shoe" dates back to Victorian times. See, some things never change. With the exception of the silver sixpence.

Something old reaffirms the bride's link to her family and her old life. Something new represents fortune and success in the new one. Borrowed brings good luck to a marriage as it was traditionally borrowed from a happy bride. Something blue traces back to biblical times and represents fidelity and purity. Don't ask me why they picked blue. Over time the silver sixpence has fallen to the side, and too bad. Not only does it represent wealth in a financial sense, but a wealth of happiness in the marriage.

Anything goes for old, new, borrowed, and blue, but here are some unusual ideas. The dress, jewelry, and veil can be anything but blue. Technically they can be blue too, if that's what you want to do. Obviously something you are wearing is new, most likely your gown, and something else is borrowed. I can't think of any wildly inventive suggestions in either category.

OLD: If possible, brides take a piece of lace or material from their mom's gown and stitch it inside theirs.

166   **BLUE:** The garter belt is a perfect solution, even if you have no intention of sharing it with the crowd. Or use blue nail polish for your toes.

Here's an example of something old and something new. Alabama's marriage statistics revealed the oldest groom was ninety-four, and the oldest bride hit eighty-eight. They both start as young as thirteen. While Alabama may seem like a foreign country to some of you, check out these worldwide wedding customs:

One of the most popular wedding activities in Germany is breaking things (hopefully, not hearts). Traditionally, the night before the wedding is the Polterbend, loosely translated to "Noisy Evening," when friends and neighbors went to the bride's home and broke dishes on her doorstep.

In Islamic countries, the groom wears white and the bride is dressed in red. Japan has the bride and groom sipping nine glasses of sake to officially seal their vows. The color orange has great meaning in Spanish weddings and it is traditional for the bride to carry orange blossoms either in her hair or bouquet. A Chinese tradition says the couple should marry on the half hour. This way they begin their life together on the upswing of the hands of the clock.

There are thousands of other superstitions and traditions. Some obsolete, some ridiculous, and a few worth mentioning:

Bet you didn't know that it's considered *bad luck* if:

- The bridal veil catches on fire (this may be my personal favorite).
- You let someone try on your engagement ring before the wedding.
- You wear a wedding band with stones (bad luck for who?).
- You buy your wedding ring on a Friday.
- You're late for your wedding.
- You marry on the bride's birthday (less presents for you).
- No one catches the bouquet.
- You get married in black shoes (I assume this doesn't apply to the groom).

- The groom carries his wallet on his wedding day (you can figure that one out).
- The bride drives on her wedding day.
- There's an odd number of guests at the wedding (started by someone who wasn't allowed to bring a date).

It's good luck:

- To lend your gown, but it's bad luck to be married in a borrowed gown (quite the catch-22).
- To buy the first gown you try on.
- To wear old underwear.
- For the bride to milk a cow in her wedding dress (my personal favorite).
- Not to bathe.
- To put salt in your pocket (I didn't know wedding dresses had pockets).
- To see a dove, frog, goat, lizard, or lamb on the way to your wedding.
- To get salt and pepper shakers as gifts.
- To marry on the groom's birthday.
- If it snows, hails, or rains.
- If all the bridesmaids are shorter than the bride.
- For the bride to dance every dance.

Traditional rituals can enhance any ceremony and personalize it for each couple. Again there are many examples and each of you should look within your own religion and culture. For example, there is the African-American custom of "jumping the broom," to establish happiness in their new home and life together; or the Jewish tradition of breaking a glass (modernized to a flashbulb) to ensure happiness.

Start your own, wear a family heirloom. Have the same song playing for your first dance that mom and dad did, if they can remember that far back. Don't feel compelled to follow any rituals if you're not comfortable with them.

If want to toss the garter, go right ahead. I personally never got the charm of this one. I never wanted to catch the bouquet if this was the

168 price to pay. Who wants a guy's hand crawling up your leg? Let me rephrase that; who wants a guy's hand crawling up your leg in front of an audience? As for my wedding, there was not a lot of throwing going on, no garter, bouquet, or rice for that matter. I guess that could be my tradition to pass on to my daughters. No throwing of any kind, including up, on your wedding day.

Follow your own path. Don't go overboard and try to incorporate every culture and tradition in your wedding. Otherwise you'll have to get married at the circus. As I mentioned earlier, if you were paying attention, there is one tradition that I strongly advocate abolishing: Let the bride and groom see each other before the wedding. They don't even have to speak; it's just for picture taking. It's just an archaic custom when nobody was supposed to see the bride before she became a woman. No self-respecting woman believes that marriage is equated with womanhood. I told you it was a bad idea.

30.

Mrs. Hyphen

According to *Bride's* magazine, 80 percent of engaged women plan on taking their husband's name. Though this is by no means a cut-and-dried area. It usually becomes a major issue if the bride has a career. Otherwise it doesn't usually become a major factor until children arrive on the scene.

There are options, some obvious, some ridiculous. It may not come as a surprise, but I have my own personal theory on the subject. I truly believe in the vast majority of cases (obviously, there are exceptions) that this decision is based on the name in question. Whether or not you like it. Whether or not you like it more or less than your maiden name. I know many women feel very strongly about their maiden name, they've had it all their lives, it's a part of their identity, blah, blah, blah. However, if that name is unpronounceable or the butt of many a joke, it becomes much easier to part with. If their betrothed has a great last name or vice versa, this is usually the defining factor. If his name is too ethnic or too easily misspelled, why bother?

Some men feel very strongly about this issue. If yours definitely wants you to take his name, you should respect that decision. Unless, of course, you are equally adamant. But if you are receptive to the possibility and it means that much to him then change it. Hey, if it makes him happy.

But, (there's always a but, isn't there) if you are established in a career where you are known by your maiden name, keep it. That's right, use his personally and socially, and yours professionally. He should understand the logic in that. Men today are a lot more flexible than our parents' generation. Then it wasn't even an option. Which sometimes I don't think is a bad thing. We have so many options that we drive ourselves crazy. Among them are:

KEEP YOUR MAIDEN NAME: But expect everyone to call you by his name. And you'll constantly think they are looking for your mother-in-law. This becomes more of a problem later if you have kids; they don't usually have a decision to make about their last name.

HYPHENATE: Use your maiden name followed by a hyphen and then your married name. This can prove to be a mouthful. See how it sounds together if you actually plan on always using both. This is a difficult version to maintain, and after a while most people, including the woman in question, tend to drop the maiden name. Or use your maiden name as your middle name. Of course you will pretty much be the only one aware of this, but it is a perfectly plausible compromise.

The other options are not quite as popular:

- Your husband can take your name.
- You can both hyphenate your names.
- You can use each other's last name as your middle name.
- Pick an entirely new name, either a combination of your names or something entirely different.
- Marry someone with the same last name as long as they aren't a first cousin.

I threw in that last one since I think that's as likely an option as any of those others. Though having said that, I've heard of all of these actually occurring. Not to mention one I won't even list as an option: a woman who made her husband shorten his family name, on the pretense that it was the same name as a well-known criminal's. Everyone else thought it was because it was a fairly ethnic sounding name that sounded a lot better and a lot more generic shortened. I wouldn't recommend suggesting this possibility to most men. It's one thing to keep your own name, it's quite another to suggest he change his family name to accommodate you.

I think this is a bigger issue the older the bride is. If you've lived thirty-five years with your name, it's harder to change. Since more and more women are waiting to get married, it's becoming more and more common to keep your maiden name. I always used my maiden name professionally and while it was slightly inconvenient it became problematic when we had children. It begins at the hospital when your friends can't even find someone with your maiden name in the maternity ward.

If you change your name, there are certain things you need to do to make it legal. Start with your social security card (by phone or mail) and driver's license (in person). Just the thought of going to the motor vehicles bureau may entice you to keep your maiden name. If you're not fainthearted, drive on down, but remember to bring along your original marriage certificate. Apparently there must be a plethora of women who try to fake this. There's a long list of other places, including at work, the bank, credit card companies, voter registration, and your passport. In fact, since there are so few missed opportunities to make money on marriage, someone came up with a "name-change kit." It contains all the forms and instructions necessary to go from Miss to Mrs.

It's confusing to use both names, but nothing you can't handle. Often I can't remember which name I used for an appointment or a reservation. And I have credit cards with both names and sometimes use the wrong signature. Sometimes I wonder if they think I'm some kind of criminal, and that I have aliases. (I never claimed to have an exciting life.) I was never wedded to my maiden name, nor did I feel strongly about my married name. Some women have a deep familial connection. Others are the last carriers of their family name and they hate to give it up any earlier than they have to.

172 With so much going on maybe now is not the time to make any decisions. If you're not sure what you want to do, don't do anything. Wait until you are sure. Try his on for size and see if it fits. If you change your name and then decide you want to go by your maiden name, to make it legal you need to go to court to change it back. Respect your fiancé's wishes, but ultimately, it's your name and your decision. You have to live with it.

31.

It's Raining, It's Pouring

Bridal showers can range in scale, just like a wedding. I've been to informal ones at a friend's house and others in fancy restaurants, some nicer and more expensive than the weddings that followed. Much like everything else today, showers have gotten out of hand. It's become a matter of topping the last one and spending as much money as possible. I'm here to tell you that's not necessary or even comfortable for some of your guests. This is the only chapter in which I'm not always speaking directly to you, as I assume you are not planning your own shower. Forgive me when I refer to you as the bride, in third person. You may want to share this chapter with your maid of honor, sister, or mom.

Apparently the evolution of the bridal shower dates back to the days of the dowry. The bride's father refused to provide a dowry as she wanted to marry a poor man, below her station in life. They married despite their humble beginnings. Friends of the couple showered them with gifts, to start their life together. No matter how you look at it, money is a factor in everything. Though there are ways to make it less so.

The job of planning the shower usually falls to the maid of honor and the attendants. Many etiquette experts say that family members should not host the shower. Baloney is what I say. In many cases, the maid of honor or the bridesmaids are sisters or potential sisters-in-law, and most mothers of the bride are happy to be involved. Most gals are happy for them to be involved, since they will often pick up the tab.

The only timing rule is that the shower should be held before the wedding. And not the day before. Usually it is held within the month before the wedding. While the bride-to-be is certainly busy then, it's not like the crunch time the week before, when the bride may be too busy to be showered with attention, not to mention gifts.

The only rule pertaining to the guest list is that they all must be invited to the wedding. I think it is incredibly tacky to invite women to the shower that aren't being invited to the wedding. The only exception is at the office. It is uncommon to invite all the bride's coworkers to the wedding, but since she spends so much time with these people they are often willing to participate in a wedding shower. In a way this helps them share these festivities with her rather than feeling left out of the whole shebang.

I lied; there is one more rule. Don't invite people to more than one shower with the possible exception of the wedding party or immediate family. Never expect them to give more than one gift. I know some lucky gals who have three or four showers. Which, truth be told, can be a bit much. Their friends throw them a shower. Their mother wants a shower with her friends and so does his mother. And the folks at the office can't resist. It can get a little overwhelming, but it's hard to fight city hall, and it's hard not to appreciate everyone's generosity.

I think it's better to have separate showers than to try to get everyone together in one place. It's a lot more fun to have one shower with girlfriends and not have to worry about what you say or do in front of the older generation. You know what I mean. I've also heard about Jack and Jill showers for couples. I think showers should remain the exclusive domain of women. I don't want any men in attendance; it takes on an entirely different feel.

While I'm all for surprises, I think it's easier not to have surprise showers. First of all you would need to coordinate all your efforts with the fiancé. And then you have to count on him to get her there dressed appropriately without letting on. That's not easy for anybody to pull off.

It also gives you a better idea of the guest list. If the bride knows about it, you can find out who should or should not be there. Just because her fiancé's colleague is invited to the wedding, should his wife be asked to the shower? Not every women who is invited to the wedding must be invited to the shower. I really believe they have to be *friends* of the bride, not merely acquaintances. Here's another point that may be arguable. I don't think you should invite out-of-towners that you know won't be able to make it. It's just a blatant plea for a gift. The same goes for out-of-town attendants. A bridesmaid that is coming cross-country will probably not be able to make it out the month before for the shower. She shouldn't be chipping in for it, as she is spending enough on the wedding, but she can send a gift. Just don't put her on the spot about it.

It's common for the entire wedding party to share the cost of the shower. That's why it's easier and more affordable to have it at some-one's home and just have a light spread. The attendants are already get-ting her a lovely gift; they don't need to spend even more money on a big spread. If her mom or a close relative is willing to splurge, that's another matter, but don't impose on the wedding party.

Invitations should be sent, nothing fancy. Save that for the wed-ding. This is the one place where you can note where the bride is regis-tered, and you should. It can make the guests' lives a lot easier. That's why it makes sense to register for a wide range of gifts: The less expen-sive ones make perfect shower presents.

Technically, the shower can be held anywhere—from an amuse-ment park to a restaurant. I think it's best not to go overboard, since you're all friends here, or at least her friend. She shouldn't need to be kept amused, other than silly shower games. And the bride probably doesn't need all the hoopla. Besides, are you supposed to bring the gift on the roller coaster? Have it in someone's home or restaurant where you can eat and drink, gossip and laugh.

If you're planning a party where most of the gals aren't pals with each other, then consider a theme shower to get everyone involved. It

176   sure beats a theme wedding. Anything from a sleep over to a high school theme, where you pull out those old forty-fives and play truth or dare. In a perfect world the best shower theme would be a slumber party, where you can regress and talk about boys and stay up all night. That sounds like fun to me.

It can feature the bride's profession, be it a lawyer, doctor, or editor. I'm not sure how you would incorporate certain professions, but you could substitute hobbies or interests. It can have a European theme or some other geographical location. Everyone can come in Oriental garb and eat sushi, if that's their bag. Or there is my personal favorite—just come as you are. Have we become so mindless that we need outside stimulation and can't just chat with these gals? Don't answer that.

There are other less complicated themes that involve the presents. As we all know, the best part of the shower is opening the gifts. Make sure someone keeps a complete list of who gave what. And I suppose it is a tradition that won't die, though it should, that someone should collect all the ribbons and put them on a paper plate for the bride to wear. Always a stunning look. Anyway, some themes include:

ROUND-THE-CLOCK SHOWER: A time is printed on the invitation and the gift must pertain to that hour. It gets a bit more complicated if it's two o'clock, either A.M. or P.M., but you can't go wrong with pajamas on one hand and a manicure on the other.

LINGERIE SHOWER: Everyone provides something sexy for the boudoir.

KITCHEN SHOWER: Everything from soup to nuts, usually not the actual foods.

ENTERTAINMENT SHOWER: All recreational gifts from novels to movie tickets to gift certificates to gourmet dinners.

ROOM OF THE HOUSE: Everyone is assigned a particular room with obvious duplications unless you live in a mansion.

WISHING WELL: In addition to the main gift, everyone brings a small item, with a little note attached. Variations on this theme can include gifts for the groom or items a bit more bawdy in nature.

RECIPE SHOWER: Everyone brings a recipe and can even **177** include the actual ingredients.

WELL-STOCKED BAR SHOWER: Something of the alcoholic nature or beautiful wine glasses or funny napkins. What's wrong with a blender and some margarita mix?

I'm certain there are many other ideas, just bear in mind the personality of the bride and the groom. If they aren't drinkers then the bar idea obviously isn't a good one. If they love to ski, consider incorporating that or another sports related theme. Just personalize it. Nothing could be more embarrassing than picking something that doesn't relate to the bride.

Let the games begin. No matter how old or mature you are, it's virtually impossible to have a shower without playing some silly games. The most conventional one is writing down what the bride-to-be says when she opens each gift. From "Isn't that cute," to "I've always wanted one of those." Then the list is read as phrases she would say on her honeymoon. It's funnier in practice than principle.

Other ideas include games with a winner. Of course you then must supply appropriate gifts. These include:

Q & A ABOUT THE HAPPY COUPLE: Ask the bride beforehand for some information and then prepare a quiz to see who really knows their history and secrets. Bear in mind you are honoring the bride, not trying to humiliate her; well, not too much. A variation on this theme is to ask her fiancé some questions, print the questions and answers on the cards. Each guest then asks the bride her questions and whoever receives the most correct answers is the winner.

WORD ASSOCIATION GAMES: One example is that everyone keeps a list of their first response to certain words. At the end they see how many matches they have to the bride. This can actually be pretty funny if you pick the right words in the first place—go for the racier ones.

MADLIBS: Write a true story about the happy couple and substitute key words. You remember how to play, don't you? Then read the story back, complete with your guests' contributions of adjectives, verbs, and nouns.

I've heard of everything from the guests weighing their pocketbooks to designing gowns made out of toilet paper. The truth is that anything goes. Again, it should reflect the playfulness, or lack thereof, of the bride.

Listen up, I'm talking to you again.

Have a good time, have a few laughs and enjoy the company of your girlfriends. Oh, and let your fiancé know that it's kind of a tradition for him to arrive at the end, with his own gift.

FUN FACTS

Did you know that there is wedding insurance? Check out your or your parents' homeowners policy. Some insurance companies offer Private Event Coverage that deals with everything from postponement to illness.

You can also have a night out with girls, but that is never quite as elaborate in nature. In fact, you should have a night out with them as a single gal for the last time. Vow to keep that tradition alive as a married lady. One tradition we would like not to keep alive is the bachelor party. Somehow this is the hardest one to kill. While I realize this is not the domain of the bride or the attendants perhaps you can use your influence, to a point.

If you don't trust his friends to keep this party in check, make sure it is held at least a week before the wedding, to give everyone an opportunity to recover. If they plan on getting drunk, make them promise not to drive. Take away the keys, rent a hotel room; volunteer your apartment and *you* rent a hotel room. Have them include both dads, tell the best man that it is very important to your father. At least that way you'll have an authority figure there, and maybe he can rein them in. Or at the very least keep them from losing total control. Appeal to your dad's strictest side, the one where he gave you curfews and grilled your prospective dates, and ask him to act as a moral conscience. If they won't invite your dad to the real party afterward, at least your brother or one of his friends might appeal to reason. In some cases you can threaten your fiancé with _____(fill in your own blank); that might get results, Not every guy has a knockdown, drunken bash. But enough do. And there is always one clown in every group, you know—that buddy of his that you are often tempted to strangle.

I'm the first one to admit that there is nothing wrong with a good time. Just make it clear to your fiancé that if he is mature enough to get married, he is mature enough to survive this night in one piece. You should go out too, so you don't stay home worrying the whole time. Most guys are responsible, and I'm sure your guy is too.

Both sexes can have a great party, and try something different. A day at the races, a weekend in Vegas or Atlantic City (just don't gamble everything you got). You can go bowling, roller-blading, golfing, scuba diving or bungee jumping, whatever strikes your fancy. If you're a sports nut only in the armchair sense, get tickets for a game. Go club hopping if you want to drink, dance, or watch scantily clad performers of either sex, but have a limo waiting to take you from spot to spot. You can have a lot more fun, and a lot more alcohol, if you don't have to worry about driving, let alone parking. Anything goes from a weekend cruise to a trip to the circus. Girls (and guys) just wanna have fun.

32

The Love Nest

The wedding is under control, the honeymoon is all set. What happens when you get back? Unfortunately, reality strikes. The biggest issue is setting up a home. Even if you've already lived together, it's just not the same. Did you share a bank account before? Do you plan on sharing one now? Does he automatically expect you to act like a wife in the worst sense of the word, as in shopping, cleaning, doing the laundry?

First things first. Where will you live—his place, your place, or "our" place? In the old days, you both moved out of your parents' home into your new abode. Those days are long gone, and I truly hope you have lived on your own before your marriage. It's hard enough getting used to being married, but if you've always lived with dear old Mom and Dad this would be a culture shock. If he has a fantastic apartment with enough closet space for you, then you're set. Of course, you'll have to scrub the bathroom and add your feminine touch to the furnishings, no doubt.

If you move in together or start anew, you will have to resolve a few areas beforehand, primarily furnishings and finance. Do an inventory of all your stuff; this will also help at the bridal registry. Decide whose stuff is better and what stuff you are going to get rid of. Try to get this all

182 together before the wedding. Ideally, you will return from your honeymoon to your newly established home. Odds are that neither of you has a ton of stuff, and most of it is junk. Where you can afford to, start fresh. Pick out things together. Try not to go for the quick fix. Wait for sales and buy the items you really want. Another LIFE LESSON down the road.

You're about to become an official couple. Even if you've been living together things are about to change. For some reason, that marriage license has great psychological as well as practical impact. It affects everything from filing your tax returns to filling out a million forms, checking married instead of single.

Wherever you land, one or both of you have to go through the change of address routine. The post office provides a free change of address kit. Keep track of all your moving-related expenses and receipts; some of them may be tax deductible. The IRS has a booklet with that information and it may be worth your time to read it. Make a list of all the companies and people that need to be notified. The master copy of your guest list would come in pretty handy right about now. And don't forget your insurance company, especially since you will need a new homeowners or renters policy. Then there's motor vehicles, subscriptions, the bank, et cetera. Don't forget about all the paperwork for your job. Are you going to keep your own health insurance? Check them both out to see which provides better coverage, reimbursement, and cost.

The area of finance is much murkier. For some reason women are conditioned to let men handle the money and the bills. Many feminists would argue that's unreasonable and women are just as capable. I know women are just as capable, but I would argue this logic. This is one of the few areas of responsibility where men will rise to the occasion. If he is happy to pay the bills and balance the checkbook, you should be happy to let him. It's one less thing for you to worry about. Obviously you should be aware of your finances and not be blind to your bills. But it is really one big headache. I thought getting rid of this responsibility was one of the real bonuses of marriage. Just don't let him think he controls the purse strings. I assume you're working and contributing to the household income. Don't fall into this male-dominated version where you have an allowance and he controls all the money.

Many couples keep a joint bank account, but don't give up their own. This way they have one account for shared household expenses and another for their own personal well being. Work this out between yourselves. If one of you is a spendthrift and the other is anything but, you'll have to balance that out. You've probably dealt with this through-out your courtship, but now some real compromises will have to be made. Like saving for the future. Obviously there is a solid middle ground to be had. If you're not there yet, work on it. Nobody said this was going to be easy. If you don't already know this LIFE LESSON, now is the time to learn it: Money is at the heart of most problems. Most tensions in a marriage are caused by money or lack thereof. I'm not saying that you have to be rich to have a happy marriage, far from it. But you have to have a clear understanding of your financial situation and of both your views on the subject. For some reason we'll be more open about sex than money. Well, now is the time to let your feelings out. You've often heard that marriage is a big compromise, and nowhere is that more true than with your money.

33

Table for Two

One of the last tasks you will have to deal with before your wedding day is the seating chart. There is no right or wrong way to handle this. The one area open to interpretation is the head table. Where are the bride and groom going to sit?

There are five basic options:

TABLE FOR TWO: The bride and groom sit alone at a small table in the center of things.

DAIS: The bride and groom sit in the middle of a long table surrounded on both sides by the wedding party.

HEAD TABLE: The bride and groom sit at a round table surrounded by their wedding party.

HEAD TABLE II: The bride and groom sit at a table surrounded by their immediate family.

HEAD TABLE III: The bride and groom sit at a table with their parents.

Let's discuss. I always thought a table for two was strange, because if one of them was sitting there by themselves they looked like a loser. At least if they are at a larger table there is usually someone else there.

186   If there wasn't, it still didn't look that awkward. On the other hand, how often do you get to sit down anyway? My friend argues that this was the rare time where she got to sit with her new husband and share a private moment.

I am not a big fan of the dais either. You can only talk to the person sitting next to you, and the wedding party can't sit with their dates. So everybody winds up leaving the table anyway.

A round head table is the way to go. Whether you go with your family or friends is a personal decision. I choose the wedding party, which usually incorporates your siblings anyway. Let everyone sit with their dates, don't separate them. This way your parents can sit with their siblings or close friends. I think everyone has the best time with this arrangement.

Now for the hard part, the rest of the guests. Figure out how many tables you will need, and confirm whether they will seat eight or ten. Wouldn't it be fun to do the entire seating for ten and find out each table sits eight? Put each couple or person's name on a piece of paper or a Post-it note. This way you can move them around without constant erasing. You will undoubtedly have last-minute changes, but try to get the seating pretty much finalized at least a week early. Believe me, this is not what you want to be doing the night before your big day. Some tables are a breeze; the neighbors from your block can all sit together. I think the (for lack of a better term) "old folk" shouldn't sit with the "kids." I don't mean children when I say kids. Pretty much anyone over twenty shouldn't have to sit with their parents.

It's a nice idea if your parents sit with his parents, space permitting. Often, aunts and uncles have come in for the wedding and they would like to sit with their siblings (your parents). All this changes if your parents are divorced, and/or remarried. If you're inviting them all, ask both sets of parents how they would like the seating arranged. Of course, if yours say they would like to sit with his parents, and his parents want to sit with their siblings, then you're in a bit of a bind. While you're asking, don't make any promises.

Don't automatically group your relatives together. If you think your aunt might really like someone in his family, put them together. Sometimes both sides never meet unless thrown together. If family feuds exist this is not the time and place to patch them up. Sit them as far apart as possible, in separate rooms if you could arrange it. If you really do have separate rooms, make sure important people of all ages are in both rooms.

The same goes for your friends. Think about it before you seat all your high school friends together. Maybe some of them would mix well with his college pals. Don't have separate tables for your friends and his friends. Many a successful match has been made at weddings, so consider the single guests carefully. Don't have one single person at a table with all couples. That could be really uncomfortable. She is better off at a singles table rather than with a group of married couples even if she knows them all. We've all heard of couples that met at weddings; what beginning could be more romantic and auspicious?

All children should sit with their parents, even the flower girl and ring bearer, unless you have a children's table set up with a babysitter or two in charge. This table should also have kid stuff for them to play with and to eat. Try paper and crayons, bottles of bubbles, and anything else that is washable and won't cause a gigantic mess. This is the only table you should purchase favors for, a goody bag of kid stuff to eat and play with. It won't cost much, but will make their day. Dare I suggest that this may be the highlight of the wedding for them? In fact, if you have lots of kids, consider hiring extra babysitters, either to stay with them in a separate room or to watch them at the party. This way the parents can enjoy themselves, and when the children fall asleep a babysitter can watch them in a private room. If the reception hall allows this possibility, go for it. Many parents would be happy to cover the babysitting costs, so ask them if they want you to make those arrangements. It is time and money well spent.

You can please some of the people most of the time; and most of the people some of the time. But you can't please all of the people all of the time. Someone will always have reason to complain. One way to avoid a common complaint is to have the "kids" near the music; the older guests tend to complain it's too loud or noisy.

188 Don't forget that once you have completed your table arrangements you'll have to write out everyone's table assignment card. If you want to assign the actual seats at the table, you will have to prepare those cards and lists, as well. Instead of the traditional numbers, people are introducing more creative concepts, incorporating themes or listing specific places or dates that have resonance with the couple. If you find table numbers mundane, go for it. I personally don't have a problem with them.

FUN FACTS

**Ceremonies can feature a Unity Candle.
The symbolism being the uniting of two families.
Both sides have a small taper and they proceed to the
unity candle to light the flame. It usually begins with the
mother of the groom, followed by the mother of the bride.
This is usually done as they are escorted up the aisle in
the processional. Then the bride and groom together light
the candle. I don't believe it is appropriate for the musical
accompaniment to be "Come on Baby Light My Fire."**

One last thing to bear in mind: Your table should be the center of attention and placed appropriately. On either side should be your parents' table, relatives, or very close friends. You don't want to be surrounded by people you've only met on one previous occasion, do you? Well, I suppose that depends on your friends and family.

You'll have ample time to admire your handiwork as you and your husband will be parading around from table to table, greeting your guests and thanking them for sharing this special day with you.

34

Practice Makes Perfect

The rehearsal dinner is the good part, but first, you have to actually rehearse the ceremony. It may sound ridiculous; after all, you just show up, walk down the aisle, and say "I do." Right? Well, it's a bit more complicated than that, which you will realize at your rehearsal. Better late than never. This way you'll be able to iron out the kinks before showtime.

Everyone involved should attend: the entire wedding party, including any children (with adult supervision), both parents, and anyone else involved in a special reading or song. If you have a wedding consultant, for the whole shebang or just for your wedding day, bring her along to answer any last-minute questions. If possible, have your videographer there to get a feel for the setup; and your musical accompaniment to familiarize everyone with their cues. Check in advance if they will expect an additional fee.

Confirm the rehearsal time with the ceremony site and your officiant. Usually this is held the evening before the wedding. And then it's on to the dinner. Finally, something paid for by the groom's side, so eat up. Though these days it can be hosted by the bride and groom. As you can imagine, I advocate that it be the domain of the groom's parents.

190   The dinner should be located conveniently close to the ceremony. You don't want to have to travel far to get there. The guest list should be limited to the wedding party members and significant others (if their date is invited to the wedding, they are welcome here), siblings, and parents. If a close friend is in from out of town, an exception could be made. If you have a relationship with your officiant, invite them along. Otherwise keep this group as small as possible.

It can be held at home or at a restaurant. With everything else going on it is usually easier to go out, but this is up to the groom's parents. Unless it is a small group, the restaurant menu should be chosen in advance. The bride and groom should have some input on these decisions.

It is traditional for the best man to toast the happy couple. I don't see the need for this unless this is his idea of rehearsing for the wedding toast. This is a perfect opportunity to give your gifts to the bridal party, especially if it's jewelry that they might want to wear the next day. It is also the perfect time to thank all the parents for their encouragement, love, and support. Just gloss right over the bad stuff. Give everyone a copy of the wedding day schedule you have prepared so everyone knows when to be where and doing what. (More in the Main Event chapter.)

That's pretty much it. The ambience can be as formal or as informal as you choose, from a five-star restaurant to a clambake on the beach. So enjoy yourself, appreciate your friends and family, and relax. Oh, one last thing, don't stay up too late; you have a big day tomorrow.

35.

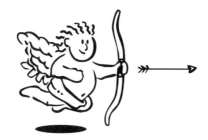

Boy Is My Face Red

Everyone loves to hear other people's most horrible and embarrassing moments. So here are some real doozies, which I hope none of you experience.

A woman whose boyfriend had dumped her learned of his upcoming marriage. She found out where he and his fiancée were registered, went in pretending to be the bride, and changed everything. Need I mention she chose the ugliest, most useless stuff, in the most horrible colors? Of course, the happy couple didn't find out until they got their presents.

A musician relates this story from firsthand experience: "One time I was doing a gig and one of the bride's distant uncles died at the reception. It was a Sunday and they couldn't move him until the coroner got there, which took about two hours. The family didn't want to lose the money they'd spent on the reception, so they covered him up with a table cloth and put a partition around him. People were literally dancing two feet from his head."

This one will teach you not to try anything fancy: A couple was planning to make their grand entrance as husband and wife from an underground platform in the center of the dance floor. Instead of lifting them

192 up in a smoke-filled fantasy à la Sigfried and Roy, the elevator contraption broke and they were stuck there for two hours. But the party went on without them. . . . One bride who was having her reception on a boat fell into the water as she was boarding. They had to wait two hours for an emergency dry cleaner run to get the dress cleaned and dried up.

Photography horror stories abound. I've heard everything from no film to forgetting to remove the lens cap to broken cameras. In one case, the photographer's insurance company paid for the bride's immediate family to fly back from Sweden so they could at least have still photos.

FUN FACTS

When you buy your disposable cameras for each table, make sure you buy the kind with an automatic flash. Some have to be constantly reset, and won't be; then you'll be left in the dark.

Here's the reason winter weddings are less popular: the weather. One couple couldn't reschedule their wedding due to the massive ice storms because the groom had to report back for military duty soon. The minister backed out (the mayor filled in), and the ceremony and reception site couldn't open. In fact the entire region was under a state of emergency. The mother of the bride went to her local grocery store to buy provisions for any of the guests that actually showed up. The good part was that they let her cut ahead of the line. While she was there, she threw in some disposable cameras as well. You guessed it, no photographer. Ultimately there was a wedding minus only one attendant. You know how they say it's good luck if it rains on your wedding day? Well, at that rate they should have some charmed life.

There's a cute story in Robert Fulghum's book, *It Was on Fire When* **193**
I Lay Down on It, about one wedding at which he officiated. This was an
extravaganza of immense proportion. Every detail was planned and
nothing was spared, including the bride's mother, when the nervous
bride threw up on her.

Here's the pièce de resistance, which was found on the Internet.
Credit was not given by name, as you'll soon realize why. This was a
large, lavish wedding of close to three hundred people. At the reception
the groom grabbed the microphone. He proceeded to thank everyone for
coming and for their love and support. He especially wanted to thank
the bride's family for the elaborate reception.

As a token of his appreciation he had a gift for everyone. If they
reached under their chairs, they would find an envelope taped to the
seat. Inside was an 8 x 10 picture (no mention of color or b/w) of the
best man having sex with his new wife. He stood and watched everyone's expression, especially (I imagine) that of his bride and ex-best
friend. He then turned to his best man and said "Fuck you" and to his
wife he repeated "Fuck you." He then left the room.

Oh, he got the marriage annulled the next day. Why, you ask, did
he go through with it? One reason: *revenge.* This way the bride's family
had to foot the hefty bill for the entire "affair." And what better revenge
than public humiliation in front of everyone important to them? I
haven't found anyone who was actually at this wedding, but I can't
believe anybody could make up a story like this.

I tell these stories not to scare you. And not just because I find them
hysterical. No, I tell them to help you relax. Odds are nothing like this
could ever happen to you. But if they do, be sure to send them to me so
I can include them in the next edition. Just kidding.

36

D Day (D Is for Diet)

The moment you've planned for, waited for, hoped and dreamed about is finally here. Take a deep breath, a good stretch, and let's get going. Let's start with a good breakfast. No, I'm not kidding. I hope you've been eating healthily up till now. Don't tell you me you're not hungry or you're too nervous to eat. No matter what time of day you are getting married, you need to keep your energy level up all day long. You don't want the first thing you eat all day to be hors d'oeuvres, accompanied by lots of alcohol. Did you imagine yourself slurring your words on your wedding day?

Even if you're not actually running a marathon (come to think of it you kind of are), this is a good time to carbo load. Carbohydrates boost your energy and reduce stress. They produce a chemical that acts as a relaxant. So *mangia*. Eat lots of small meals in the week leading up to your wedding. During this last week and especially on D day, take it easy on salt, alcohol, and caffeine. Drink plenty of water, especially on your wedding day. This will help flush out that alcohol so you don't pass out. The downside is extra bathroom breaks, but it will give you a chance to sit and relax, alone, for a minute.

196   Basically it's all common sense. All the nutrition rules you've ignored up till now should finally be incorporated into your lifestyle this last week. It's not going to make you feel like a different person, but it should make you feel better and help you have more energy and less tension. Which is just what you need. If someone told me that by eating healthier I would feel better and be less stressed on my wedding day, I would jump all over it. So should you.

Make sure you have a healthy snack right before you slip on that wedding gown and are about to recite your vows. On top of your nerves do you want to feel lightheaded or, even worse, faint up there?

37

The Clock Is Ticking

You're in the home stretch. You've made it this far, one more week to go. Hang tough. There is still a lot to be accomplished. If you have extra vacation time that's not going toward the honeymoon, take off the last few days. If not, do you get personal days? If you can't, settle for really long lunches.

By now you should have had your final fitting for your wedding gown and should be picking it up this week if you haven't already. You and your fiancé should have applied for a marriage license or plan on doing it any day. The rules vary from state to state, so find out about the applicable waiting periods in yours; contact your local government offices.

You should finalize and confirm all the arrangements with your assorted wedding vendors. From the band to the florist to the honeymoon (from sea to shining sea), it can't hurt to double-check. This, by the way, is a perfect example of what a wedding consultant could do for you.

Plan on charging everything that day, but check the fine print first. Some contracts call for the final payment to be cash, check, or money orders. Confirm your final guest count with the caterer. If some of your

198   invitations have gone unanswered call up the rude parties and ask them point blank if they plan on attending. Refrain from commenting, "When were you planning on letting me know?"

Get a manicure the day before. Don't wait until D day. You'll be busy and nervous enough without worrying about smearing your nails. Just make sure you have an extra bottle of the polish for emergency touch-ups. Keep it with the truckload of emergency stuff you should be putting together. This list covers almost every possible contingency. Hopefully you won't need any of it, but for peace of mind. . . In one bag you should have the following, feel free to add anything extra:

- aspirin
- tissues
- chalk (touch-up for shoes and dress)
- sewing kit with scissors
- safety pins
- bobby pins (white and brown)
- colored nail polish
- clear nail polish (stocking runs)
- makeup
- extra pantyhose
- tampons or napkins
- Scotch tape
- Band-Aids (blisters from the new shoes you didn't break in)
- bottled water with straws (keep that lipstick looking good)
- hairspray
- antistatic spray
- comb or brush
- mints
- nail file
- change (pay phone)
- cell phone (charged)

Keep all this together in a place that is private yet easily accessible during the reception and ceremony. Keep an extra lipstick in your groom's pocket. If there's anything else like allergy medicine or Valium, throw it in.

Also prepare a master list of everyone involved in the wedding and their phone numbers, from the members of the wedding party to your photographer. Bring along copies of your contracts, so there can't be any dispute.

Do you have a lot of out-of-town visitors? An attendant, a favorite aunt? While I'm not one to create busy work, if you have the time and inclination, put together a little welcome basket for their arrival, or have the hotel help you out. It can be there waiting when they check into their hotel. Fruits, sweets, wine, whatever you want. Put in a personal note welcoming and thanking them for coming. Perhaps you could include some information on local attractions and good restaurants, with phone numbers. Put in your number and both your parents', in case they need to contact you. If you have fifty people, this may not be such a hot idea, but for a select few it would set a lovely tone.

If you're not having limousines especially for the bridal party, arrange transportation for the out-of-towners. If there are enough people staying at the hotel, consider renting a minivan or bus. If you need to set up rides, put your mom on this task; she can get her local friends to help.

Give your attendants their gifts, if you haven't already done this at the rehearsal dinner. If you still haven't found the perfect gift, what are you waiting for? Try to get something personal, and while it doesn't have to cost a fortune, don't be cheap. Think about all they've spent on their ensemble. Here are some suggestions:

- Jewelry: the traditional choice.
- Gift certificates: A day of beauty, local bookstore, restaurant, makeover, or even a personal trainer, unless that's too personal.
- Magazine subscriptions.
- Engraved stationery.
- Pay for their bridesmaid dresses.
- Take them away for a girl's weekend.
- Pajama party, and you provide the pj's and slippers.
- Spring for a hotel room the night before, or of, your wedding.

- The day before, treat everyone to a manicure/pedicure and lunch.
- Pay for everyone's makeup and hair that day.
- Go shoe shopping and surprise them by buying the shoes.

They all sound good to me. Try something unique that fits your friends and your price range. If you plan on getting your future husband a gift, it's now or never. It may as well be never. Sure it's nice, but does he really need another watch? What else could you get him? Isn't enough time and money being spent? Would he really notice? It's hard enough to find gifts for their birthdays and anniversaries. You'll have your whole life to buy him ties and briefcases, so pace yourself.

If you haven't already had a dress rehearsal, now's the time. Put everything on that you plan on wearing to your wedding. From the stockings to the garter. Practice walking around, great time to scuff up those shoes. You can always use sandpaper. Have your mom or MOH practice bustling the gown and helping with the veil.

Pick a friend or two. One of them can be assigned to the photographer to assist him in pointing out all the people on your must-have photo list. Delegate responsibilities to other friends, from picking up the flowers or checking them out when delivered, to giving Grandma a ride to the ceremony. Your parents will be a little crazed that day, too, so don't look for their help until afterward. I know a part of you is groaning, Do I have to do everything? Well, yes. You don't actually have to *do* everything, you can delegate.

Some of the jobs to delegate could be:

- Have someone drop your suitcases off at the hotel where you will be spending your wedding night.
- Arrange for someone to pick up your wedding dress and tux from the hotel the next day.
- Make sure the tuxedo is returned to the rental store or, if it's his, brought to the dry cleaners along with your wedding gown, for cleaning and preserving.
- Assign a point person for your wedding day to act as your power of attorney. Make certain that it is someone you trust

implicitly to make decisions so you won't have to deal with last-minute minutiae.

I think you get the idea. Give this some thought ahead of time. Ask for help and assign specific chores. Nobody can refuse a bride in her hour of need.

Run through the chain of events (if you haven't already) with the MC and/or bandleader. If you want the bridal party announced at the reception, type out a list of names. If they are difficult to pronounce, write them out phonetically. It's embarrassing to mispronounce the best man's name.

If you don't want any or all of the reception rituals, speak now or forever hold your peace. From dancing with your dad to cutting the cake to throwing the garter, decide what you're keeping and what you're losing. Don't wait until that moment to inform them of your decision.

Make lists. Write down every possible problem or situation that you can imagine. If they are important enough, work out some type of contingency plan. You have that master list with all the names in case you need to contact anyone concerned with the wedding. Don't worry, relax a little bit. Think about all the things that will go right and don't worry about all the things that can go wrong.

38

Toast of the Town

There's no getting around it. Toasts will be made at your wedding. The only "mandatory" one is by the best man, though there are no rules against others toasting you as well. The only rules are that they be short and sweet.

This is part of the reception time line and the bandleader will announce the best man's toast. You will have a clue that this is about to happen by the fact that the waiters are filling the champagne glasses. Even though most people will only take a sip, it's the thought that counts. The best man often comes center stage with the bride and groom and says something clever, witty, and, best of all, personal. There is usually a reason why someone is the best man, and they should be able to come up with something better than the generic "Here's to the bride and groom, wishing them a lifetime of health and happiness, yadda, yadda. . . . "Not that there's anything wrong with that, but the best toasts are the ones that come from the heart. Here's a cute idea, if the happy couple can take a joke. A best man made his speech and talked about all the women who would have to get over the groom. He then announced that all the single women who had keys to his bachelor apartment should come up and return them. The best man had given out keys to all the single women beforehand, so a whole parade of gals marched up on cue.

204 It got quite a laugh, but we all know some women don't have a highly developed sense of humor or do have a highly developed sense of mistrust. Just be careful who you pull this one on.

Whoever intends on delivering a toast should plan ahead. Your drunken friends shouldn't take turns standing up and babbling on. They should come up with a personal toast and have a practice run. Make that a dry run, without the champagne. Don't stand up if you have nothing to say. If the best man needs some ideas send him to the library. There are plenty of books on toasts, and if he can't be original, at least he can sound intelligent. The other standard toast is often done by the groom, toasting his in-laws for the beautiful affair, as well as his parents, and thanking all the guests for coming, on behalf of himself and his bride. The father of the bride may deliver a similar toast, thanking all the guests on behalf of his wife and himself for sharing in this celebration, and making some clever, and possibly humorous, remark to the groom about taking care of his daughter, or else.

Of course, there are rules about toasts. You're supposed to raise the glass in your right hand, and clink them together before drinking. As the toastee, you are supposed to sit there smiling and graciously acknowledging this toast. I personally think it's better if you are standing near the toaster (not the one in the kitchen) as it makes for a great photo op.

The other part of this tradition is the clinking of the glasses. This dates back to the old fashioned belief that the sound of bells (I guess this was as close as they could get) would scare away the devil. Every time the guests clink their glasses the bride and groom are supposed to kiss. It's cute the first couple of times, less adorable the next few, and downright annoying if they continue. As the bride, you can't really scream at your guests to knock it off. However, there are some variations on this theme:

- Not only do the bride and groom smooch, but they pick another couple at random. One way to accomplish this is to have a bowl or bag with slips of paper, pull out a name, and turn the tables.
- Instead of making noise with their glasses, your guests use their vocal chords. Have the bandleader announce in advance that instead of clinking, the guests have to stand up and sing a song with love in it.

39.

The Main Event

It's finally here: *your wedding day.* Congratulations, you made it. We knew you would. I hope the weather is perfect, but don't worry if it's not, that's supposed to mean good luck. Not to mention frizzy hair.

You have plenty to do today no matter what time you are getting married. Stay in bed a little bit longer, this may be the last peaceful moment of your day. Try to eat something even if food is the last thing on your mind. You need all the energy you can get and breakfast may have to sustain you for the better part of the day.

Hopefully you've followed our advice and planned ahead so there is a lot less to worry about. You should have prepared a schedule to help things run more smoothly. If you're an obsessive compulsive, you have detailed everything to the synchronized minute. If not, it's still a good idea to have some basic order to follow. Let everyone do their jobs. Don't try to help or even observe; you don't need the headache. That's why you hired professionals, they have done this before. Remember you're the virgin here.

If you're doing this on your own or you have hired a consultant, you should adhere to a schedule. Undoubtedly you will not be at your sharpest today. For some reason you are in a fog, and can barely remember what

206 you had for breakfast, let alone when everything is supposed to happen. A little preoccupied today? That's why your schedule should include every mundane thing you can think of, not to mention every mundane detail that you want the wedding party to follow. Everyone from the best man to the photographer should get a copy of this time line. Hand it out at the rehearsal. This schedule should also include master phone list, including cell phone and pager numbers, so you can track anyone down, if need be. *Everyone* involved in the wedding should be on this list.

Here's a sample schedule for an evening affair:

KIM AND PETER'S WEDDING TIME LINE

11:30 A.M.	Kim and her wedding party arrive at the Plaza. With *the dress* and accoutrements, and Kim and Peter's luggage for honeymoon.
12:30	Kim and rest of wedding party go for hair appointments.
2:00	Girls return to Plaza for room service lunch.
2:30	Makeup person arrives to begin ladies' makeup.
3:00	Florist arrives.
4:30	Photographer arrives. Takes photos of the wedding party getting ready.
5:00	Entire wedding party arrives at Hotel and meets in Salon A.
5:15	Designated person or consultant distributes bouquets and boutonnieres.
5:30	Family portraits are taken in the park. Refer to specific list of photos.
6:00	Formal photos taken of wedding party in Grand Salon.
6:30	Videographer arrives.
6:45	Band arrives and begins setting up.
7:00	Officiant arrives at hotel.
7:15	Kim and Peter sign marriage license.

7:30	Guests begin to arrive.
8:00	Ceremony begins in Grand Salon.
	Prelude music begins.

Processional order:

Rabbi

Debbie and Mitch

Jane and Evan

Fern and Steve

Justin (best man)

Peter with his mother and father

Maria (maid of honor)

Dylan (ring bearer)

Lucy and Josie (flower girls)

Kim with her mother and father

8:30	Ceremony concludes.
	Receiving line: Bride and Groom and parents.
8:45	Guests proceed to cocktail reception.
9:30	Dinner in Grand Ballroom.
9:45	Kim and Peter are not formally announced. Instead the band will play their song, "It Had to Be You," they will enter room, and begin dance. No specific parents' dance.
10:00	Kim's father makes welcoming toast. (Note: Provide cordless mikes for toast.)
	Appetizer served.
10:15	Dance set.
10:30	Salad is served.
10:45	Dinner is served.
	Soft background music is playing.
11:15	Best Man's toast.
	Kim's brother's toast.
	(Note: no garter belt or bouquet toss.)
11:30	Band returns.

208

12:00	Bride and Groom cut the cake.	
	Band plays immediately after cake is removed.	
12:15	Coffee and cake served	
12:30	Last dance set.	
1:00	Celebration ends.	
Note	Cars to transport parents home arrive at 1:00. Kim's mom brings gifts home.	

Kim and Peter keep envelopes (dying of curiosity) and bring them to their honeymoon suite at hotel. Flight is not until tomorrow evening, so they will have a brunch with wedding party and close relatives tomorrow. They will give envelopes to her parents for safekeeping. Her mom will also take her wedding dress to be cleaned and preserved, and the best man will return Peter's tux. Whatever you do or wherever you go immediately after, it is vital that you make arrangements for your dress and the tuxedo. If it's not rented, bring it to the cleaners with the gown.

Obviously every wedding is different, so your time line should reflect that. The point is to have a schedule and for everyone to have a time frame. It will be quite an accomplishment if you can stick to it. But if you start off on the right foot, you should be able to pull it off.

If you want to send thank-you notes with a wedding picture, ask the photographer to take a separate roll of you dancing or cutting the cake. That way you can get it developed earlier instead of waiting for your wedding pictures.

Even if you are leaving the reception, you don't need a special going away outfit. Since you are staying until the end, odds are very few of your guests will be hanging around. It will just be close friends and family. Make sure you bring something to change into for the ride to the hotel or airport or home. You don't really want to jump into a taxi in your wedding gown, do you?

Make sure you and your groom take a quiet moment to savor this party. Go to a private corner and watch the action for a minute and enjoy the moment until someone swarms in on you. Many couples wish they had taken a moment to capture the festivities.

40.

The Bride Cuts the Cake

These are all optional, just decide if you want them or not.

- Do you want the guests to sign a guest book? If so, have one set up by the place cards as they enter the reception.
- Decide if you want bandleader or MC to formally introduce the wedding party or announce the Bride and Groom for the first time as a married couple for their first dance.
- Decide if you want mother/son or father/daughter dances. If so, pick songs. Doesn't have to be "Daddy's Little Girl" or "Thank Heaven for Little Girls" or "Sunrise Sunset." Again the possibilities are seemingly endless, another detail to think about. Listen carefully to the words to make sure the song is appropriate.
- It's traditional (and entirely optional) for the groom to dance with his new mother-in-law and the bride with her father-in-law. Then the maid of honor and best man dance, followed by the rest of the wedding party.
- Provide cordless microphones for toasts.

- Let the band know if you want any special music played. At Jewish weddings, the first set usually involves the hora and traditional dancing.

- Are there any special religious blessings you want, done by a family member or the officiant from the ceremony? Let the MC know in advance, so he can announce it.

- Do you want a cake cutting ceremony? Or do you just want the photographer to take some pictures and not make it a public event?

- Do you plan on throwing the garter belt or bouquet? There is an alternative for the bouquet to be given to someone special, married or not. The bride can give a little toast to that woman and present it to her, not throw it at her.

- Do you or the groom want to make a special toast to your parents or guests?

Feel free to add ten more items to this list if that is what you want for your reception. These are just some of the more traditional aspects to consider.

Another incredibly important, yet unspoken aspect of the reception, is the gratuities. Who do you tip, when, and how much? Who will be handling this for you? Have your cash allocated in advance. There are no hard and fast rules here. Some contracts automatically build in gratuities, so check first.

41.

Thanks a Million

If people truly wanted to give you a gift you would genuinely appreciate, they would add a PS to their card saying no need to send a thank-you note. What greater gift is there? This is not what you want to deal with when you're in your post honeymoon state of euphoria. Granted, after a week of work, laundry, and the real world that phase will have passed. But the last thing you want hanging over your head are those thank-you notes. Especially the ones in which you have to find something nice to say about the hideous gift they sent.

As with everything concerning this wedding, it's better to deal with this sooner rather than later. The quicker you get it done with the happier you will be. Simple logic. It's considered bad form to send thank-yous later than two weeks after receiving the gift. I wouldn't stress out about the timing, just bear it in mind so you don't think you have all the time in the world.

The other rule that I think should be broken is that only one of you should sign the card. Probably only one of you will, since the overwhelming odds are that you are writing *all* the thank-you notes. Yet another area your new husband will wash his hands of. Many couldn't really care less about proper etiquette rules. Sure they want to acknowledge the gifts, but isn't that women's work? I don't understand why it is considered improper to sign both your names. Probably some etiquette doyenne, undoubtedly a woman, was so pissed off at her husband after writing two hundred thank-you notes, that she instituted this rule. While I can see where she is coming from, you may as well present a united front.

The etiquette police suggest the alternative, that you mention your husband in the note. Something like "Jerry brings me fresh flowers all the time and we always use your beautiful vase." "Sam loves wolfing down the candy I put in your fabulous bowl." "Max loves spending the money you sent." How stupid does this stuff sound? So you are supposed to rack your brain to come up with something clever to say injecting him into the scenario as well? Talk about adding insult to injury. It's not enough we have to write them in the first place?

Enough whining, you have to write the notes so get moving. If you ordered your thank-yous with your invitations you're in business. If you had the envelopes addressed when you wrote out the invitations you are golden. Aren't you happy you did? Pull out that master guest list, which should be annotated with everyone's gift. If you don't have thank-you notes, don't use regular stationery, there's too much room to fill. Find the smallest note cards you can. You'll thank me later.

Try to write with some feeling and appreciation. Initially, this may not prove difficult, but as you continue you will experience major burnout. Stop writing. You don't want to send a card that says "Thanks for that really nice thing you sent. Thanks for coming to the wedding. See ya." I realize by this point you are drained, but that doesn't diminish your guests' generosity. If it takes more than two weeks, that's fine. It's better to be sincere than to be speedy. Except if you hate the present; then it's better to be insincere. We all know that certain people are more concerned with protocol than others. Send them their thank-yous first. Then move down the list until you get to your friends who realize you have a life and better things to do with it. It's not that you don't appreciate and want to thank them, you do. You just don't want to do it right now.

Use that nice pen you bought for the invitations; it will make this **213** more special for them and for you. The most special part will be using the pen to check the names off the list. While you're at it, this is a good time to send a thank-you to the people who helped at your wedding. If someone went above and beyond the call of duty, it's a nice touch to send them a note. Certainly it's a nicer touch to give them a big tip, but this doesn't hurt either. I know you aren't trying to increase your workload, sorry.

FUN FACTS

Ten Missouri legislators recently introduced a bill rewarding newlyweds with a cash prize of $1,000. The requirements are: Both the bride and groom must be over twenty-one, test negative for sexually transmitted diseases, and have no prior marriages or children. Oh, and the woman must not have had an abortion.

Remember it's the thought that counts. If they thought enough to send a gift, you should think enough to thank them promptly with sincerity and enthusiasm. Your work is now officially over, though your guests technically have a window of a year to send a wedding gift. Which means you may be doing this for the better part of a year. Odds are overwhelming that most of your gifts will come with your wedding day. So don't think you can procrastinate for a year. You don't have that same window of opportunity to acknowledge the gifts.

Hope you had fun and had a great time at your wedding. If everything went well, I hope your marriage is equally successful. If not, look at the bright side: Things have to get better. While it's difficult enough to offer advice on planning a wedding, I don't pretend to have a clue as to marriage. Let me know when you find someone who does.